PROTECTING ÇATALHÖYÜK

PROTECTING ÇATALHÖYÜK

Memoir of an
Archaeological Site Guard

Sadrettin Dural
with contributions by Ian Hodder
Translated by Duygu Camurcuoğlu Cleere

Left Coast
Press Inc.

Walnut Creek, California

Left Coast Press Inc.

LEFT COAST PRESS, INC.
1630 North Main Street, #400
Walnut Creek, CA 94596
http://www.LCoastPress.com

Library of Congress Cataloguing-in-Publication Data

Dural, Sadrettin, 1953-
    Protecting Çatalhöyük: Memoir of an Archaeological Site Guard / Sadrettin Dural ; with contributions by Ian Hodder ; translated by Duygu Camurcuoğlu Cleere.
        p. cm.
    Includes bibliographical references.
    ISBN-13: 978-1-59874-049-3 (hardcover : alk. paper)
    ISBN-10: 1-59874-049-0 (hardcover : alk. paper)
    ISBN-13: 978-1-59874-050-9 (pbk. : alk. paper)
    ISBN-10: 1-59874-050-4 (pbk. : alk. paper)
1. Dural, Sadrettin, 1953- 2. Private security services—Turkey—Employees—Biography. 3. Çatal Mound (Turkey) I. Hodder, Ian. II. Title.
    GN776.32.T9D85 2006
    363.28'9092—dc22

2006033267

Cover photo and author photo by Jason Quinlan. Maps by John Swogger. Stamp seal drawing by Ali Turkcan. All provided by kind permission of the artists and the Çatalhöyük Project, directed by Ian Hodder.

Editorial Production: Last Word Editorial Services
Typesetting: ibid, northwest

Printed in the United States of America

∞™The paper used in this publication meets the minimum requirements of American National Standard for Information Sciences—Permanence of Paper for Printed Library Materials, ANSI/NISO Z39.48–1992.

07 08 09 10 5 4 3 2 1

Contents

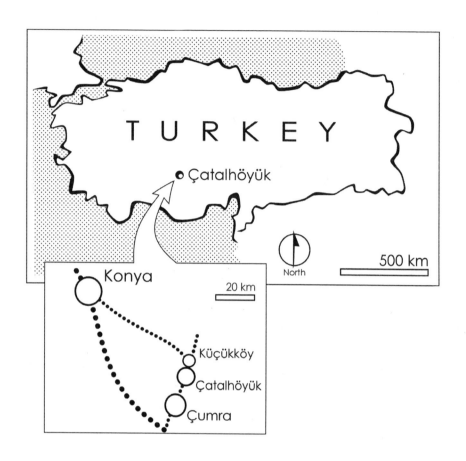

TURKEY

Çatalhöyük

North

500 km

Konya

20 km

Küçükköy

Çatalhöyük

Çumra

Foreword–*Ian Hodder*

I first met Sadrettin at the site of Çatalhöyük. It was our first season in 1993. Sadrettin was ever present as we tried to work out how we could live and organize our lives in the early days. I could understand very little of what he said. My Turkish was very poor, and he spoke in a very fast jumble of words and with a thick local accent. He smiled a lot and made people around him smile. But it was not until much later, when I could speak a bit more Turkish and he had found some tapes to learn English, that I really got to know him and to appreciate his wry view of the world. I taught him about the site so that he could guide people around the site better, and because he just wanted to know. He had this appetite for knowledge. But I also taught him because I wanted to know his slant on what we were doing and how the site might be interpreted.

It seemed wrong that his perspective, his voice, should not be heard. Other villagers were part of the team and took part in our discussions, and their voices are heard in some of our publications (see especially Hodder 2005c). But Sadrettin's role as a guard, having to be ever ready to take a tour around the site, meant that he was on the margins of the research we were doing. And yet he became such a central part of our lives, a real personality in our midst, looking at us from his background in the village.

I was amazed, but pleased, when he said he wanted to write a book. Having seen so many pictures of the "local workforce" adorning the pages of the great archaeological tomes from the Middle East and elsewhere in the world, and yet never having read a word written by these people who made archaeology possible, and who spent sometimes many generations working as field archaeologists or site guides, it seemed important to encourage and help Sadrettin in his venture. He had never used a keyboard before and could not understand why the letters were not in alphabetic order—many moments of hilarity followed as he poked fun at the insanity of the jumble that he had to learn.

The text that Sadrettin produced was an outpouring of consciousness, but also of fun, anger, and hurt. When I first saw the Turkish text, it was about 50,000 words in sequence with not one paragraph, full stop, comma, or capital letter—just a long stream of words. With the advice of some friends of the project, especially Nurcan Yalman, Ayfer Bartu Candan, and Can Candan, we asked Sadrettin to make some changes to focus more on the site and his time as a guard there. Once he had made these changes, Duygu Camurcuoğlu Cleere did a quite remarkable job of translation. Sadrettin's text was difficult and unconventional, with many local colloquialisms. She managed to capture his style and wry humor, and in correcting the English I have as far as possible tried not to edit the resulting text. The device of using notes seemed unobtrusive while allowing me to provide some explanation and context for the reader, so as better to understand Sadrettin's meanings.

So at last I began to see what our presence meant to Sadrettin, from his point of view. I saw how we had intruded ourselves into a rich and complex world of knowledge about the landscape and about the ancient mounds that dotted the Konya plain, of which Çatalhöyük is just one of many examples. I saw how wrong it was to say that we as archaeologists had "discovered" these sites, when all we had done was to recognize their significance in terms that made sense to us. I realized more fully how local people became dependent on us, but we were so rarely there for them. We came and went seasonally, extracting what we wanted for ourselves. I understood more clearly the lack of sensitivity that we and tourists bring with us.

I wanted to let Sadrettin write in his own voice, and I

have perhaps already said too much. But I do want to thank some people, beyond those already mentioned, for making this book possible. Shahina Farid, as always, gave advice and support. Indeed, the excavation team as a whole has been part of the process whereby Sadrettin felt involved in what we were doing. I also wish to thank Mitch Allen for having the courage and vision to make this book available.

Sadrettin's is not a success story. It does not chart the successful education and empowerment of one of those many who have for so long been overlooked at the edges, but actually at the center, of archaeology. It could hardly be said that Sadrettin's story charts the end of centuries of colonial archaeological manipulation and silencing. His story is at once amusing, uplifting, tragic, and unending. But in providing us with his voice, Sadrettin has opened up new possibilities for dialogue. I have learned a lot from him in terms of how Çatalhöyük might be managed and interpreted, and in terms of how archaeologists might work with local communities. I hope that others, too, will gain from reading his words.

Preface

I was born in Küçükköy, a small village near Konya in Turkey. Even though I wished to study after I graduated from Küçükköy primary school, I lost my chance of further education due to the lack of high schools in my village. As I started working at Çatalhöyük, my desire for studying and learning increased. I was impressed by the knowledge and the education of my archaeologist friends who came from different parts of the world, and this made me more aware of my situation. I started training myself as I listened to the stories of the excavation team as well as the visitors. I also had many memories. Therefore, I decided to write a book in order to share these memories which came from my personal experiences at Çatalhöyük. However, I was worried about writing this book. As I am not well educated, some people may think that I am not able to write a book. Even though you may come across many mistakes, I really wanted to share my memories with you and therefore worked hard to complete it without making many mistakes. Please consider the level of my education while you read this book. Greetings to everyone!

Sadrettin Dural

1 Beginning my new job at Çatalhöyük

Before the year 1993, I was working as a taxi driver in Konya, near the village where I grew up. I was married, with two children, and was having serious financial difficulties looking after my family. The days went by and one day my father called me to the village saying that İsa Ferli, the old guard of Çatalhöyük, was retiring and if I was interested in his position, I had to apply to the Konya Museum. But what was Çatalhöyük? It was a Neolithic settlement which was founded nine thousand years ago. I immediately submitted my application to the museum. I didn't hear anything from them for a while, so I asked my father to go to Konya[1] to find out what was happening with my application. When he arrived at the museum and introduced himself as my father, the director[2] told him that they hadn't been able to reach me and he was pleased to say that I was offered the job. My father was very happy, so he asked the director what he could do to thank him. The only thing the director said was I should guard Çatalhöyük with great care and always help the visitors.

When my father told me the good news, I can't tell you how happy I felt. I tried not to cry. It was sunset and I was sitting on the balcony. My wife brought me a cup of tea and I remember thinking that the sun was smiling at us as it was disappearing in the sky. It was telling me that my problems had now come to an end. Then my father told us to pack up our stuff, since we were moving back to the village. I was going to start work at 8 the next morning, but it wasn't possible to fall asleep with all the excitement.

I went to bed at 4:30 in the morning. My wife woke me up at 7 and warned me not to be late for the government duty.[3] I had my breakfast, got my lunch box, and left for Çatalhöyük. When I arrived at the site, I saw İsa Ferli's brother who said that İsa went to Konya to get his pay. It was the 15th of February 1993. My old work partner Mustafa came in the evening and told me that he and the old guard used to have a work plan according to which they swapped guarding the site every week. He asked me if I wanted to carry on the same way and I said okay. Then Mustafa left and I made myself a cup of tea, had my dinner, and left the guard house. It was snowing and there was nobody around. There was a little woodstove in the room and the smoke coming out of the chimney was calling me in. I went into the house. There wasn't anything to do. The radio was on but I started feeling a need to talk to someone. I hung around for a while, got bored, and decided to go out again. However, it was pitch black. I thought, If something happens to me, nobody will know! The trees were making noises to scare me and the little guard house was hiding itself as if it knew that this was my first night. A fox was howling close by, saying that he was the king around here. I said to myself that this was my first night and that was why I was feeling this strange fear. Just then, I heard a truck approaching and suddenly felt secure. I wished the truck would come here but it drove toward the village and disappeared. Now there was only Çatalhöyük and me. It was midnight when I went back to the guard house. I laid on my bed and tried to calm myself down. I must have fallen asleep. Suddenly I woke up with a terrible pain, feeling that someone had slapped me on the face. I got up and turned the light on. There was no one around. Then I realized what it was. It was a Yatır! Yatır is a dead person who didn't commit any sin during his life and therefore he is allowed to live both in this world and in the afterlife.[4] I know that you don't believe me, but it couldn't have been anyone else.

It was 3:30 a.m. I thought that the previous night I couldn't sleep from the excitement, but tonight I wasn't able to sleep from fear. What was going to happen to me? If I worked as a guard, I was going to get beaten up. And if I carried on being a taxi driver, then there was no way that I could afford to look after my family. Believe me, I seriously considered both options and decided in the end to get beaten up by the Yatır. I decided that I would bring my wife the following night. I wouldn't tell her that I was scared, so she would encourage me unknowingly. As these thoughts were going through my head, I heard the call to prayer. Then I fell asleep. I woke up again when the alarm went off. My brother came to visit me. He asked me if I was feeling okay, since I was looking very pale. I told him to bring my wife in the evening.

My wife arrived in the evening. She tidied up the guard house and we started chatting as we had our dinner. I wanted to tell her how I felt last night, but I didn't know how to start. When I said to her that I needed to talk to her, she looked into my eyes and asked what was wrong with me. I knew that even if I told her the truth and gave up this job, I would still have to guard the site that night. This would only scare her. Therefore I decided not to tell the truth and instead told her that this job wasn't as easy as it looked. There was nobody around to talk to and if something happened to us, nobody would know! So it was best to carry on as a taxi driver in Konya. She said that she would support my decision, but asked how I could so easily forget the difficulties we had in Konya. There were times when we couldn't afford to buy any bread. When our kid became ill, we had to use the medicines that the pharmacist gave us, since we didn't have enough money to go to the hospital. We ran out of coal in midwinter once. She was right, how could I forget that moment?! It was March. I was working as a taxi driver. I came home at night to have some food, and found my wife quite upset. I asked what was wrong. She said that there was no coal left. The house was freezing and we had a nine-month-old baby. We were both worried that our baby was going to get ill. In the meantime I was trying to think of a way to warm up the house. Eventually I decided to go to the car and take out the spare tire. I released the air and cut it into pieces to burn in the stove.

Now, at Çatalhöyük, my wife reminded me of the problems we had dealt with in the past and told me that I had a better job now and I should use this opportunity by working very hard. The job may be difficult and I may get upset, but our life in the past was harder than today. The future of our children depended on me and hence I should not think about myself but my children. I totally agreed with her and decided that even if I died, I would not give up this job.

I wanted to go to bed but my wife stopped me, saying that the night was long and it was early to sleep. It was around 10:00 p.m. She made some tea and we talked for a while. There were two sofas in the room. I laid down on one and she was on the other. The children were staying with my mother in the village. Even though I was feeling very tired, I couldn't go to sleep. I was thinking about what my wife had said. I couldn't leave this job. I had to secure the future of my children. Suddenly my wife woke up and shouted at me, asking who slapped her on the face. I knew who it was but I didn't say anything. She looked at me in anger as if I slapped her. I was also quite confused. Despite being awake, I did not see anybody doing it. I must have fallen asleep while I was thinking these things. My wife woke me up in the morning. She was smiling. I was still alive and this made me feel very happy. She wanted to go back to the village, since the kids were with my mother. I asked her to tell my mother to visit me.

My mother arrived in the evening. After a long talk, I told her that I was scared of this place and asked if she could pray for me. She comforted me, saying not to worry. When I woke up the next day, I realized that I didn't get beaten up during the night. After breakfast, my mother decided to leave. I asked her to stay one more night, but she refused. She was quite upset, since she couldn't sleep all night. I asked her whether they beat her up, too, but she said no and started walking toward to the village.

There I was on my own again. I started thinking how I could manage to spend the night alone and decided that alcohol would be the solution. I started drinking two or three glasses every night before going to bed, and it helped me to build up my confidence. The days began going by quickly. I was spending one week at Çatalhöyük and one week in the village. Three months later, I found out that a new excavation was going to get started at Çatalhöyük by an archaeologist named Ian Hodder. I was very excited, since this meant that the excavation team was going to arrive soon and it was going to be great to meet and talk to them.[5] I started imagining how it would be to work when they were around, where they would sleep, eat, and relax. The little guard house wasn't big enough to accommodate these people. Europeans aren't like us, I thought. They like their comfort, so they would probably set up something new. I also imagined what kind of people they would be. Now you may say that I am a guard at Çatalhöyük and many foreign tourists are visiting the site. So why am I very curious about the excavation team? You are right; however I started working at Çatalhöyük in winter and there were no tourists then.

The first visitors arrived in spring. I was in my guard house studying English when I heard the noise of the first tour bus. I left the house immediately and couldn't believe my eyes. They were all Japanese, except the tour guide and the bus driver. I used to watch karate movies, so I knew that Japanese were very good at it. They all looked like Bruce Lee. As we were touring around the site, I remember being amused by them. They all looked like each other, as if they were born from the same mother. Since they were the first tourists I ever guided, I always remembered them.

Days and months went by and yet there was no news from the excavation team. One day, Osman Ermişler from the Konya Museum and a person called David from the British Institute of Archaeology in Ankara came to Çatalhöyük to gather workmen to work for the excavation.[6] They asked for our help to find some workmen from the village. They told us that the team was going to arrive soon and start excavating with the help of the workmen. While we waited for the arrival of the excavation team, a friend from the village called Rıza Büyüktemiz came to visit the site. He was one of the workmen who were going to work here. As we were chatting, I asked him whether he thought there was a Yatır at Çatalhöyük. Even though I didn't mention what I had experienced, he said that there was definitely a Yatır at the site and carried on telling his story. There was a field opposite the site which belonged to his family. In 1984, he was putting a fence up and was on a tractor. It was about 11:00 at night. He saw the Yatır going from Çatalhöyük to a mound called Tekke. He became very scared and started running. I asked how many they were. He couldn't remember, but said maybe three or four people. I asked what they looked like. He said that he couldn't see their faces, but there was a silhouette of their bodies. I asked him why he ran away. He said that he was very scared.

I got worried again and tried to tell myself that I could drink more tonight to be able to spend the night at the site. But what about the excavation team? Maybe there would be no time for me, as the Yatırs would beat the whole team up. Poor people, I thought! Even though I had done nothing at the mound, I got beaten up so many times. These people were actually going to excavate here, so only Allah knows what would happen to them. They were lucky however, because they were going to stay in Çumra, not at Çatalhöyük.[7] When I found out about this I felt happy, since it meant that they weren't different from us at all. I felt closer to them when I met Ian Hodder. When he asked us if they could use our kitchen to make tea at 9:30 a.m. and noon, we said that we could make the tea and serve it for them. Every day at 9:30, we would make the tea and the team would come down to our guard house, together with the food which they would bring from Çumra. You wouldn't believe how tired they would be. They would all sit around the floor due to the lack of chairs in the house and I used to think how different they were than I expected. They were always very polite even when they thought they were hassling us asking for more tea. Soon, we started seeing these people as our friends, sisters, and brothers. We always made sure that they wouldn't come across any problems around here. We used to get very worried when we saw them tired. They were people like diamonds, as we say in Turkish. Our love and respect for these people has increased day by day and aged like the Neolithic houses of Çatalhöyük but has never been diminished.

The excavation was now over and it was going to carry on next summer. Since the team was leaving from Çumra, I couldn't see them before they left. Feeling quite sad, I used to go around the trenches they worked at and imagine their arrival at tea time. It seemed like Çatalhöyük was crying behind them. I felt lonely again. Who could I tell my problems or dreams? Who could I serve the tea for? I kept wondering if they missed me, too. They were gone and we were left alone with our Yatır, trees, and foxes. It seemed like there was nothing else around to do. This loneliness wasn't going to be permanent, I thought. They were going to come back next year as if they had never left. Therefore I had to wait. Tourists were going to start visiting soon and I was going to guide them.

I kept thinking about these things. One day, a group of foreign tourists arrived at Çatalhöyük. They told me that they were priests and one of them said he lived in İzmir. I immediately told them my story about the Yatır and asked if they would pray for me. They walked around my room and prayed. I am sure you are wondering if the praying was useful at all. I really don't know. The only thing I know was that I was drinking more and more before going to bed.

Every day was the same. Sometimes, one finds it hard to understand oneself and then starts remembering the past. It seems we always appreciate the past but never the present. I believe that next year I will remember today with its sweet memories. I wish that every one of us could have a nice life both in the past and the present. Following these thoughts, I would like to share a memory from my youth. I was 22 and single. My friend Mevlüt and I decided to go to the city for a day.[8] We were going to visit a female friend called Gülşen. We got off the dolmuş and walked to Gülşen's house.[9] When we arrived, I rang the bell and suddenly her boyfriend started shouting and swearing at us. It was hard to listen. Mevlüt couldn't stand this and started swearing, too. He was calling him downstairs. It seemed like we were going to have a fight. We couldn't believe our eyes when Gülşen's boyfriend opened the door. He was huge! We both stood frozen where we were. Mevlüt had shut up, but the guy was still swearing. I tried to tell him that we were looking for the religious house but he told us to get lost. We left the place and walked quite a while without talking to each other. We were both very upset. Then I had an idea. I told Mevlüt that there was no reason to get upset, since we could find a friend as big as him and he would sort him out for us while we rescued Gülşen. Mevlüt asked me if I knew anyone like that and I suggested Mehmet, a friend from our army years.[10] The only thing was to persuade him to do it for us and I told Mevlüt to leave it to me. We got on the dolmuş and went to Mehmet's house. He offered us tea and asked what was wrong. I started telling the story, because I thought Mehmet would only listen to me. However he said that this had nothing to do with him, since Gülşen wasn't his friend. I tried to persuade him by saying that he was my friend and if he helped us, Gülşen would also be his friend. He asked if Gülşen would like him and I told him that she liked big guys like Mehmet. Then he asked if she was pretty and I said if she wasn't, we wouldn't go to this trouble. I described her as if she was the most beautiful girl in the world. Mehmet joked, asking why a girl like that would be friends with us. I pretended that I was offended and Mehmet seemed persuaded.

I described Gülşen's friend as a small-featured guy. Mehmet wondered why we couldn't handle him if he was small. I tried to get out of the conversation and asked him if he was going to help us or not. Mehmet asked us to follow him and finally we arrived at Gülşen's house. I rang the bell and the boyfriend started shouting and swearing. We were also swearing and calling him downstairs. Suddenly, the huge, fat guy came out. Mehmet turned to me with anger, realizing that I had lied to him. I told him that last time I saw him, he was skinny. They started fighting. Mevlüt and I were laughing. The fight didn't last long, since Mehmet was trying to get out of the fight. Once he was free, he started running away. We were following Mehmet as the fat guy followed us. I thought that if we couldn't reach Mehmet, we were in danger. Then I heard Mehmet shouting at me that I put him into this trouble and he was going to take his revenge. He stopped and started walking toward me. Since I felt that he was going to beat me up, I started running away. We didn't talk to each other for three months following that day. I was quite upset after what happened, but now I remember it with a smile on my face.

2 Excavations begin–
The team settles in

One morning I was guarding Çatalhöyük, when a taxi arrived at the site. The visitors told me that they were the architects and came here to build an excavation house.[1] I was very happy, because this meant that the excavation team was going to stay on the site and we were going to be together during the excavation seasons. I took the architects to the place where the house was going to be built. After a short time, the building work started under the supervision of a representative from the Konya Museum. The plan was to complete a section of the house at the end of each year. Even though I was very excited to know that the team was going to stay on the site, I couldn't help wondering what they would do when they got beaten up by the Yatır. Unfortunately, I couldn't help them. They would work during the day, relax in the evening, and then would be beaten up by the Yatır.

Finally the excavation team arrived. I thought that they were always going to remember their first night on the site. The next morning, I waited on the path where they would walk up to the site. I wanted to see if they were okay. With my little English, I asked how they were, but they all seemed happy. Nobody was complaining about the Yatır. It isn't fair, I thought. Why was I the only one who got beaten up? I was only guarding the site, but the team was digging the mound. So, they should get beaten up more. Besides, they would only believe me if they got beaten up, too. I wasn't lying. Rıza had also seen them. I knew that the only way not to get beaten up was to drink more alcohol, so I kept drinking.

It was a very hot day. One of the builders came to the guard house. He said that he was ill and asked me if I had any medicine. I checked the first aid cupboard and couldn't find anything. Then I remembered having those chocolate sweets called Bonbons. Without showing the box, I gave him one with water and told him that this was a very expensive pill which was brought from Europe. He was slightly suspicious because of the color and asked why it was like that. I said that the pill itself was very bitter, so they covered it with sweetener. Therefore he must only swallow, but not chew it. He took it and left. While I was wondering whether what I did was good or bad, he came back and told me that he was feeling very well and asked if I could give him another one for later. I gave him another one and told him that it was the last one. In the evening, I went to the builders' house to visit him.[2] He was looking well and praying for me. I was very embarrassed and wondering how this guy could get better with a chocolate. He was either not very ill or my chocolate pills presented a miracle. I remember experiencing something similar to this.

It was before I started working at Çatalhöyük. My female friend and I went to the beach. As we were sitting on the hotel balcony, watching the sea and sipping our beers, I was thinking how pretty a little boat looked in the distance. I guess I must have felt very emotional, since I ended up drinking quite a lot. Soon enough, I started having a terrible headache. We were planning to visit some friends that evening, but the only thing I wanted was some painkillers. I asked my friend if she had any and she told me to look in her bag. While I was looking for the painkillers, I found these strange looking pills which I thought might have been newly released. So, I took one. After a while my friend asked how I was feeling. I said that the pills she had were very strong and healed my headache instantly. When we came back to the hotel, my friend told me that somebody had been in her bag. I told her that it was me looking for the painkillers. She disagreed with me saying that it couldn't be me, since it was a woman. I asked how come she knew it was a woman. She said that one of her contraceptive pills had been taken. As she showed them to me, I realized that I took the wrong pills. I had to admit it even though my headache was long gone. She laughed and told me that, apart from headaches, I was probably protected against babies, too.

The builders were really nice people. One of them was from Trabzon and had one younger and two older builders to help him. When I arrived at their place, they were getting ready for the work. I asked one of the older builders called Ali to sit down and relax, since I could work for him instead. He refused my offer, saying that he came here to work and he would only feel happy if he worked hard, with no help from me. I thought he was right. It wasn't possible to survive without working and once you were appreciated by others, it was the best feeling ever. I was very lucky in this case. I have been always appreciated both by Ian and by my boss, the director of Konya Museums, Erdoğan Erol. Now I want to tell you about one of the thousands of favors that Erdoğan Erol did for me.

It was winter. One morning, I woke up and realized that I became hamamcı. You are probably wondering what hamamcı is. If you have sex with someone in your dream, it is called hamamcı. In Muslim religion, if you have sex either in your dream or in real life, you must have a shower afterward. Therefore I had to have a shower as soon as I got up. However, the only shower was outside. There was no shower in my little guard house, but only a small toilet. Although it was very cold outside, I tried to take a shower. The next day, I was ill. It must have been the cold shower that I took the day before. I decided to go to the doctor. I had a permission letter from the Konya Museum which needed to be signed by the director. I knocked at Erdoğan Erol's door. When he saw me, he asked what was wrong, since I was looking very ill. I told him that I had to take a cold shower the other night, but didn't know how to tell him that I had been hamamcı. I tried to whisper. He became very angry, asking why it happened and whether I looked at women's legs. I swore that I didn't.

He believed me and signed the paper. I went to the doctor and got better in a short time. The director then had a proper bathroom built in the guard house. I really appreciated that. I realized that we weren't working hard for nothing. He was looking after us. We all liked him. I was very lucky to have a boss like Ian Hodder and a director like Erdoğan Erol.

One day, I was sitting in my guard house when I saw Uncle Mehmet coming from the field. I called him over thinking that we could have a nice chat. He asked for a glass of water as he sat down. He was very old, but still working hard in the field. He used to work in Germany. When his finances got better, he decided to return to Turkey and started working as a farmer. Unfortunately, he lost his first wife soon after he moved here, but then got married again. When the second wife died, Uncle Mehmet was worn out.

He sighed while looking at Çatalhöyük from the distance. I asked what was wrong and he started talking. He told me that when he was a kid, they used to work and play here, since nobody knew about Çatalhöyük.[3] The old times were different. Suddenly he wanted to leave. I asked him to stay and told him that I would take him back in my car. I asked him to talk about the old times. He said okay and carried on telling a story:

> When I was young, we used to own a wheat field. From morning till night, we used to plough the wheat with the help of a düven. What is a düven? It is a wooden vehicle about 2 meters wide and 3 meters long. Despite being very tired, I couldn't relax when I came home to rest. There was the right type of wind that night. So, I went back to the field and carried on plowing the wheat.

While Uncle Mehmet was telling his story, I stopped him and asked why he went back to the field that night instead of in the morning. He laughed, saying that plowing the wheat when there is the right wind is very important. He carried on:

> When I finished working, I fell asleep in the field. When I woke up, I was very affected by the dream that I had that night. In the dream I was told that if I dug the soil around the tree that was on the well behind the hill,[4] I was going to find a pot of gold. I didn't dig the soil, but told my dream in the local coffee house.[5] Youngsters who had heard about my dream had gone to the field to find the gold. On the first night, they couldn't find anything except a tree trunk. On the second night, they went back and this time they started digging the mound. Suddenly, they heard some people shouting: "They are digging Çatalhöyük!" Our youngsters started running away and when they looked at the mound from the distance, they saw strange silhouettes of people. The next day, they went back to the mound to check the footprints of the strangers, but the only thing they could see was their own footprints. They have never gone back to Çatalhöyük.

After his interesting story, Uncle Mehmet wanted to go home and I gave him a lift. I was quite confused after his story. If there were people who protected Çatalhöyük, how come they let James Mellaart discover and excavate the site in the 1960s? Did they protect the site for thousands of years and then decide that 1958 would be the year to discover the site? I was wondering if there were people still guarding the site. If not, who was beating me up at night?

3 My routine as a guard

Days and nights, winter and summer were chasing each other as I was guarding the site. I believe that the warm days are followed by the cold winters and every day is ended by a night. Therefore we have to be strong. I had really difficult times in the past, which I will talk about in this book. It is important to know that each night is also followed by a day, and the bad times are followed by the good times. So we should not lose our emotional strength and we should never give up. We must believe that we are never alone. If we feel lonely, we must think about our mothers, fathers, children or even our cat. If we live far away from our loved ones, we must look at a mountain or a tree, which will make us feel closer to the people we miss. I want to tell you a story regarding these feelings. A man goes to a psychiatrist and says that he feels very depressed. The doctor asks if anything happened to upset him. He says that he woke up with his wife screaming, "Don't kiss Hasan, don't kiss!" The doctor says that this is a good thing as his wife is thinking about him even in her dream. Then the man says that his name isn't Hasan, but Ali. The doctor thinks for a few seconds and says that it is still a good thing, since his wife said, "Don't kiss Hasan!" What if she had said, "Kiss Hasan!" Ali sees that the doctor is right. He feels very happy as he leaves the doctor, since he realizes that his wife loves him and he loves his wife.

This story explains that whatever our religion or nationality, we will have good and bad times as long as we live in this world. I want to give an example. Ian Hodder has an assistant called Shahina Farid.[1] She is a very good friend. She always treats everyone equally and listens to people's problems. One day, when I was sitting in my guard house, Shahina came. She was learning Turkish at the time. She asked me if everything was okay. I said that I was quite upset, since my wife and I weren't talking to each other. She said that she would talk to her and try to help if I wanted her to. I was so happy. It wasn't that she offered to talk to my wife, but that she wanted to help my marriage. I didn't know that I was important for Shahina, even though I knew that we were a team with our director, students, workmen, and the guards. My respect and friendship toward her has increased as she always listened to my problems and became a good friend to me. I would refer to her as my sister and she would call me her brother. Due to our close friendship, I would often joke with her. Some evenings, I would hide outside her window while she was working. Her desk was next to the window and she would get extremely scared when I suddenly appeared. But she always knew that I was joking, so she would never get angry with me. One evening, I saw her sitting by the mound, drinking a soda and thinking. She was alone. I decided to scare her off, but she was on the other side of the fence. So I walked around the fence and went through the main entrance. I was trying to be very quiet as I was thinking how to scare her. When I approached her, I could see that she was upset. I wondered what was upsetting my sister. She seemed as if she was watching the view. There were mountains on her left which looked beautiful during the sunset. There were a few trees over the mountains and some flood lines which appeared like a newborn gazelle as they forgot their past. However, Shahina was looking at the mound. She looked very upset and unhappy which was quite different from her often smiling face. I decided not to joke this time and returned to my house. I started wondering why she would be upset. As far as I knew, she wasn't married and didn't have children. Her family was okay, too. So why was she sad? I wanted to help her, but couldn't find the right way to do it. Next morning, she looked much happier, but soon I saw that her problem was continuing. Another evening, she was sitting at her desk, watching the sunset as I was writing my book. She told me to carry on. After about 20 minutes, she started looking very sad again and suddenly I realized that she was crying. I decided to go over to her and ask what was wrong. I think that she got embarrassed and quickly wiped her face. I told her not to worry and admitted that I also cried from time to time. She felt a little relaxed, but her eyes were trying to tell me that she wanted to be alone. I went back to my desk and kept wondering what the reason for her distress might be. Did she know that the bad times were always followed by good ones?

Now I am asking you, my readers. We all experience these kinds of feelings, but do we ever realize that when we are upset about something, others become worried about us? We must share our problems, so that they can help us as far as they are able to. Nobody is alone! I am not trying to teach you a lesson here, so please don't get me wrong. Once upon a time, a man walked on a path and arrived at a water source. He drank some water and then curled up under a tree for a nap. After a while, he was woken by the noise of an old man and his camel. "Hello!" said the old man. The young man said hello back and asked where the old man was coming from. The old man said that he was coming from the downtown village and going to the windmill across the river to grind some flour. The young man asked if he was going to grind two bags of wheat. The old man said "one." Then the young man asked why there were two bags on the camel. The old man said that one of the bags was filled with soil and the other one with wheat. The young man was confused and asked why he filled the bag with soil. The old man said to balance the bag of wheat. The young man disagreed and said that wasn't the way to do it. The old man asked how he should do it. The young man got up, picked up the bag with soil, and emptied it. Then he filled the bag with half of the wheat from the other bag and said that this was the right way to do it. The old man appreciated him and asked if he was a vezir. What is a vezir? In old times, the person who assisted the governor of the country was called vezir. The young man said "no." Then the old man asked if he was a very rich businessman. The young man said that he did not have any money. The old man nodded and put all the wheat in one bag and filled the other with soil again. The young man asked what was wrong with his way. The old man said that he did not need his advice, because what he did not know was probably better than what the young man did know.

Although it seems like we can determine our lives, it isn't always possible to control things which may be good or bad for us. As we are in the flow of daily life, we forget how the small things we do can help us gain a better living. The monthly wages that I was earning at Çatalhöyük were not enough to survive.[2] I sold my car which I used to drive as a taxi in Konya and bought a new one which I also sold to a guy called Kerim Ferahkaya who was a dentist in Konya. By doing this trade, I made quite a lot of money. Then I carried on trading as I bought and sold wheat, yeast, beans, and so on. I was earning good money and thinking that I had left the bad times behind. However, the money didn't change my personality. You may ask how I can be so sure. If the money had changed me, I would have lost all my friends. I didn't lose any friends; in fact, I met a lot of new people. In buying my first car, Kerim not only made me very happy as I earned some money, but he also created a new work opportunity for me. I wanted to find out more about him, since his money brought good luck to me. When I found out that Kerim Ferahkaya was a very honest, helpful, and genuine person, I thought that the money coming from a guy like him would inevitably bring good luck. My honest trade was getting better every day and my life had become more comfortable. I had my car and, most importantly, I was working at the world-famous Çatalhöyük. I was very happy. The trade I was doing was very different from what the Neolithic people of Çatalhöyük had done. They brought a large amount of herbs (i.e., rosehip) from the Taurus

Mountains, and also stone, and flint stone, and were exchanging them for other things. According to Ian Hodder, trees were possibly brought to Çatalhöyük via the rivers.

I remember when I was a kid, we decided to demolish the sheep fold where we kept some old stuff. We found some huge tree trunks in the attic. They looked like they were evened on the corners. I asked my father if he knew where my grandfather had gotten these trees, since they didn't look similar to the types of trees we had in my village. He said that he didn't know, but he had heard that my great-grandfather would bring the trees he collected from the mountains by tying them together and setting them into the river so that they would travel in the current. This wasn't the only similarity between the Neolithic people and us. I was amazed to know that we also traded via exchange. Old men who lived in the mountains would bring things like dried grapes, white soil (in order to paint mud brick houses), and red soil (in order to paint under the varnish for decoration purposes), and our villagers would buy these things and would offer wheat or yeast in return. These traders were called çerçi. I remember a çerçi coming to our village when I was a kid. He was yelling out what he was selling. My nan told me to call him over. She bought some white and red soil and in return gave him half a bag of wheat. I wanted to get some grapes, but my nan told me that we didn't have enough wheat to give the çerçi. I started crying. The çerçi couldn't bear me crying and so he gave me a bunch of grapes. After he left, my nan told me that it was a good trade. I remember wondering what was good about it. You buy soil and give away wheat. I think that I will understand the Neolithic people better as I learn more about my own society.[3]

I was working very hard when guarding Çatalhöyük. I was guiding a lot of tourists who came from different parts of the world, but there was a big problem. I wasn't able to help them properly, since I didn't know how to speak English very well. This was really upsetting me. So I decided to improve my English. I started studying every night with the help of my English books and tapes. I was finding it difficult but I knew that I had to do it. I studied hard and soon noticed that my English was improving. I was able to inform the visitors about Çatalhöyük using my English.[4] Now I want to tell you a story about how successful my English was.

One morning a taxi arrived, while I was having my breakfast. Some people got out of the car and I told them that I was the guard here and that I would give them a tour around the site using my limited English. They seemed content. There were three people, one man and two women. I was waiting for them while they were reading the information board. The man came toward me and introduced himself. Then the women joined us. The man introduced one of the women as his wife, but I couldn't understand who the other woman was. I pretended that I understood everything they said and we started the tour. I gave them some information first, but the married couple were talking to each other nonstop. Then I started talking to the other woman who I soon realized was trying hard not to laugh. I wasn't saying anything funny, but then I thought maybe she liked laughing. As we moved on to the second hill, I started talking about the mountain Hasan Dağ.[5] I could see that they were very impressed by the mountain. Before I finished, the married couple walked away from us, giggling. The other woman was so furious that I thought she was going to beat me up. I wanted to say that there was no problem and I was just trying to give them some information. Then the man came back and they all looked like they were ready to listen to me. So I started again. I was telling them about the amount of lava that Hasan Dağ used to spray when it erupted and how the people of Çatalhöyük used this lava to make their tools. When I finished, we started walking back to the entrance. The married couple were still giggling about something. I was quite upset, since they were very rude to me even though I tried to help them as much as possible. Suddenly the single woman came over to me and after a few seconds of staring at each other, I told her that I was only trying to explain about Hasan Dağ, but nothing else. She told me that she understood and carried on saying other things, which I couldn't understand. Then she held my hand. I was trying to think how to get out of this situation while cursing Hasan Dağ for getting me into this trouble. Luckily, a tour bus arrived at that moment. I felt relieved when I saw the tour guide. I introduced myself and asked if he could help me. I told him what had happened. He then said something to the tourists I had been showing around and they said something back. He looked confused, saying that I had told them that I was in love with their friend. I tried to explain that I didn't say anything like that. The guide asked me to explain what exactly I said to them. I told him that I talked about Hasan Dağ and how it sprayed lava when it erupted and so on, but before the guide finished interpreting what I said, everybody started laughing. I never felt so embarrassed. I found out that the word "lava" in Turkish sounded like the word "love" in English. How could I know! Once the tourists realized the misunderstanding, they apologized to me.

This experience led me to think that learning English wasn't going to be very easy. But I didn't give up. I carried on studying and every word that I learned became useful while I was talking to the visitors. It was fun to work at Çatalhöyük and to meet interesting people. I was also keen on thinking about the past and listening to the stories of the elderly. Now I want to tell you a story about something that took place in the town of Karkın.[6]

Once upon a time, there was a man called Mehmet Ağa. He would often ride to the city on his horse. If he had lots of things to do in the city, then he would plan his journey back the next day. He would always take his beloved black dog with him. He would never rush when on the road, thinking that he would be back home in Karkın by night. During one of his return journeys from the city, it started raining. Even though he tried to ride his horse faster, he realized that he couldn't make it to the town by nightfall so he decided to stay at the first han that he saw. What is han? In old times, the places where travelers stopped for the night were called hans. As the rain increased, Mehmet Ağa wished that someone else would join him in this small han, but nobody turned up. He covered his horse and got ready to sleep with his dog by his side. After a short while, he heard some strange noises coming from outside. He thought that it must be evil, since his dog didn't bark to protect him. He decided to pretend to be asleep, but the noises kept increasing. Then two evil spirits entered the han and lit a fire in the middle of the room. Suddenly their number increased and they started dancing. One of them suggested making a halva. The others liked this idea and they gathered together a tray, and some sugar and flour. They carried on dancing while they made the halva. The dog also joined them. Every now and then, some of them wanted to wake Mehmet Ağa, but the others thought that if he woke, he would spoil their fun. Mehmet Ağa got up and grabbed the tray tightly, so that the evil spirits ran away, but the tray remained. In the morning, he noticed that there was no halva in the tray but some animal shit. He cleaned the shit away and brought the tray back home. Following that night, his dog wouldn't return back home. Mehmet Ağa told everyone what had happened, and apparently even today the tray is known by his grandchildren as the tray of evil.

Dear readers, it is hard to believe in this story, but it is true. It was talked about for many years and is still told today. I really believe that it happened, because there are still a lot of strange things happening in the world. Once I had the chance to watch a spiritual mass which was done by a group of tourists who came to visit Çatalhöyük.[7] Please don't get me wrong. I am not trying to criticize or make a comment on other people's beliefs, but I just want to share with you the things that amuse me.

It was summer. Lots of visitors visited Çatalhöyük on that particular day. My friend and I were guarding the site.[8]

A female tourist wanted to see the unexcavated part of the mound. In my role as guard, I approached and told her that she wasn't allowed to go up onto the mound on her own. She said that she needed to go up and suggested that we go together. I said okay. We went up the mound while her group was still by the entrance. Before they arrived, she laid out a large cardboard on the soil and asked me to let her know when they were approaching. When I told her that the group was arriving, she hid herself under the cardboard. The group circled around the cardboard and suddenly she got up and started shouting, "Mother goddess! Mother goddess!" I was also within the group and was trying to understand what was going on! The woman seemed fine a minute ago, but now she was shouting and running all around. She sounded like she had lost her mind. She was running toward other people, still shouting out "Mother goddess!"

There were always interesting groups like this visiting Çatalhöyük. I tried to do my best to make the visitors feel welcome on the site. I enjoyed experiencing interesting scenes and meeting amusing people. All in all, I loved working at Çatalhöyük and I accepted all the visitors as my friends, regardless of how strange they were. Now I want to mention another interesting visitor group. This group only consisted of women and they didn't like men. They told me that they wanted to walk around the site by themselves and I told them that it wasn't possible to visit the site without me guiding them. I could see that they weren't happy about me being around, but there was no other option. They were either going to bear with me or weren't going to be able to visit the site. As we walked around the site, some of them picked up some soil and licked it, while others were actually eating it. I was quite confused. I had been told by Ian and the museum director that the visitors must not take anything from the site. The soil wasn't included in this, but maybe it should have been, since these people weren't taking the soil but eating it. Çatalhöyük was losing its soil. As I was thinking how I could explain the situation to them, I saw their interpreter. I asked him to tell them not to eat the soil. In a very sarcastic way, he asked if it was forbidden. I said yes, because if everybody eats the soil as they do, there would be no soil left for Ian Hodder to excavate at Çatalhöyük.

I have more memories to tell you about the visitors, but I also want to talk about the interesting stories which took place around Çatalhöyük. There is a little town near Küçükköy where my mother was born. The story that I will tell you now is a true story and my mother's brothers were involved in it.

Toward the northwest of Çatalhöyük, there is a mound called "Ağa Adamı."[9] My uncles were working in a field which is about 300 meters away from this mound. When my older uncle Mustafa and the younger one Tahir had reaped the harvest, they carried it on a kağnı arabası. What is a kağnı arabası? It is a vehicle which is made from wood.[10] There is a large trunk in the middle where the wheels are attached on both sides. The whole vehicle is run by oxen. Anyhow, my younger uncle was known to be quite naughty, whereas the older one was a little naïve. Tahir would fill the kağnı arabası with crops and ask Mustafa to empty it while he collected the leftovers. Tahir knew well that Mustafa couldn't come back for at least 3 hours and thus he would sleep until Mustafa returned. Apparently they worked like that for three or four days. On one of those days, Mustafa looked very upset. Tahir asked what was wrong, but Mustafa said nothing. Tahir was sure that there was a problem and decided to empty the crops this time. After a while, he arrived at the mound Ağa Adamı. Suddenly he noticed a chicken by the road together with her chicks. He got confused and just then the chicken turned into a goat. Tahir was sure that it was şeytan. What is şeytan? Şeytan is a thing that tries to direct people to do bad things and it can be visible or invisible as it desires.[11] Tahir took out his gun and waited. The goat changed into a human. He walked toward the kağnı arabası and told Tahir to get off. Tahir shot the şeytan as he watched it dissappearing into the sky in the form of fire. He emptied the crop and returned back to the field. The next time, he asked Mustafa to empty the crop. Mustafa went and came back and nothing happened on the way. But he then told Tahir what he used to experience. Tahir realized he had seen the same thing and he told Mustafa that he had shot the şeytan.

All in all, it is hard to believe that a lot of strange things happen in the world. The world is huge and full of many different lives. However, it is important to realize that one can live how he or she wants, but without anybody else around, one is nothing.

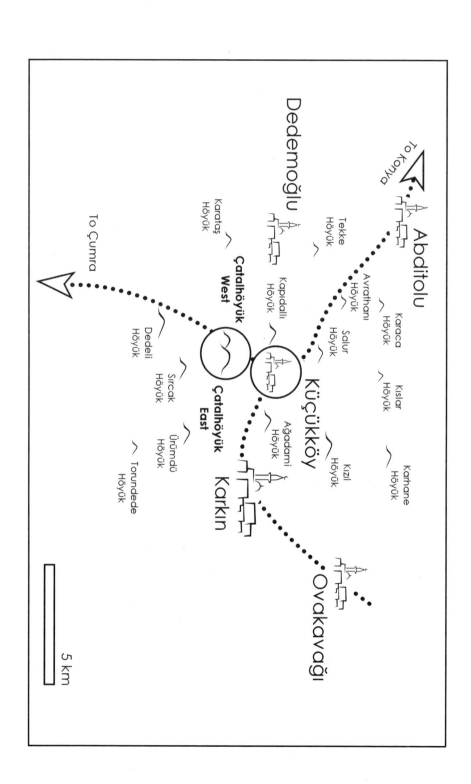

4 Loneliness and friendship among the ancient mounds of the Konya plain

In winter at Çatalhöyük, there were times when I wouldn't talk to anybody for a week. I would wish that there were a few people around. I hadn't realized until then how much I liked being with people. But did the people like being with me, too? Everyone would have enemies and friends, of course. Nevertheless, I liked everybody.

One of those lonely days, a tourist arrived at Çatalhöyük. After we walked around the site, he asked me if he could stay over. I told him that he wasn't allowed to stay on the site. Then he said that he could take his car outside and stay in it. I said okay. He parked his car outside the entrance and laid out a blanket by its side. He sat down and started eating his biscuits. I was quite suspicious, wondering why he wanted to stay here. I went to him and asked if he wanted to join me for dinner. His eyes sparkled as he walked to my house. After dinner, he rolled cigarettes both for me and for himself. He was very quiet. I offered him some vodka. He must have liked it, since he started talking nonstop and telling me about when he fought in Vietnam. I couldn't understand many things that he said, but kept saying "yes" not to upset him. It was very late. He wanted to leave, but I didn't want to let him go. It was cold outside and he was an old man. I told him that he could stay with me if he wanted. He looked very happy. I had two sofas. He slept on one and me on the other. I woke up early in the morning and prepared the breakfast. After we ate, he told me that he needed to leave, but he would come back again. I said that he was always welcome. But how would I know that he would come back that same evening?! It turned out that his wife was staying in a hotel in the city and he didn't want to stay there even though he had paid for the room. I was trying to understand why this guy preferred my little house to a nice, comfortable hotel. Obviously, he had experienced some difficult times in the past and he was still not happy with his present life.

Now I want to ask you something. Let's have a look at our present lives. Do we consider it nice or not? Let's say that it isn't going well. We will try to make it better and it will constantly trouble our mind. It isn't going to be easy to work hard in order to earn money. Finally we will have everything that we wanted. How about later? Are we going to miss our past? Will I be missing poverty when I become rich or vice versa? It is very difficult to live like that. I think a middling life style is the best option for all of us. I wish that my rich friends wouldn't envy poorness and my poor friends would reach a middle-class lifestyle. One always wants something, such as a house, a car, or maybe a yacht, and works hard to achieve it. It is actually nice to have desires like these rather than having the real thing, since the feeling of wanting something so much and getting excited as one approaches to it is unexplainable. Once we achieve what we want, the passion and excitement disappear. Therefore, it is very important to enjoy the feeling as intensely as possible before we lose it.

There would also be lives which we desire, but can never reach. For instance, everyone must have a memory of a lover. Some of us manage to get together with this person, but some of us don't. I want to give an example from my own life. I also fell in love once. She was a family friend and I was often staying in her house. Even though I was single and she was very pretty, I didn't have any personal feelings at first. She was more educated than me. One day, she asked if I could write a poem. I said that I had never thought about it, but I knew that one needed to be in love in order to write poems. And I wasn't in love, I said. But from that moment, I started feeling attracted to her. I didn't understand how it happened, but there I was in love with someone! I really loved her. I wanted to be with her all the time and you might not believe me, but I was deeply inspired to write poems. What a terrible pain it was! I didn't care about anything else but her. When my parents saw the state I was in, they called me and told me that they were planning to arrange my marriage. I rebelled and said that I was in love with someone else and I would only get married to her. My parents then refused to agree to my desires and said that I should get married to the girl they had chosen for me. My world was collapsing. I decided to talk to my father and told him that if they didn't let me get married to the girl I loved, I would commit suicide. My father reprimanded me but made no other comment.

Sometimes, I used to go to my girlfriend's place to give her the poems which I wrote for her. As she was telling me how much she loved me, my love for her was increasing. It felt like she was the source of my life. We saw each other for about a year. One morning, I woke up with a strange feeling. Birds weren't singing and the sun wasn't warming. It was a depressing day. It was obvious that something wasn't right. I went to see the girl I loved. She didn't even look at my face. Finally, I found out that she had been playing with me all that time. She led me to fall in love with her and once she had her fun, she wanted to get rid of me. Nevertheless, I have never thought anything bad of her and I am not going to reveal her name. I was in a terrible pain. She asked me if I had anything to say. I told her that I was going to say it by writing one last poem for her. I feel pleasure in sharing this poem with you which I wrote many years ago in great misery.

THE LAST POEM
I wrote my last poem for you my darling
I will not write anymore, I swore on my love
I wished to explain my love through my poems
I wished to throw away my poems that couldn't explain
  my love

You don't know what love means, but if I tell you the
   only thing you know, you will get upset
You don't love me, but the only thing you love is a car
   or fame
If I was given the same things, believe me I would refuse
   as I am in love with you
Fame doesn't bring happiness my darling, how could you
   believe that?

I asked the hodja[1] to tell me the truth
He said not to take anybody's rights with me to the other
   world
How will you pay my rights in this world?
One day when I die, don't come to my grave my
   darling, even though you fall in with me.

Even though I went through a lot of pain, this love
story is now a memory. I am married with two children
and I am very happy. What I learned from this memory
was that the heart of a single man is like an empty harbor. He would put out a light for the ships that are coming from a distance. One ship would see the light and go
toward it. This may be the beginning of a long love story.
There are hearts, however, that even if there is already one
ship at the harbor, wouldn't turn the light off, since they
would always be ready to accept others. Another ship
would arrive at the harbor and the light would still be on.
Eventually, the harbor would be too small for two ships.
One day, one or both of them would leave and there would
be nothing left from the sparkling light which used to shine
from the harbor. I want to tell a joke at the end of this
story. A boy enters the room while his father is beating
the maid. He asks his father if she has broken any plates
and is this why he is beating her. The father says that it is
worse, since she has broken his heart.
   There was an old man called Hasan who lived in my
village 20 years ago. He was a friend of my father and he
often would come to our house to have long chats with

my father. Hasan didn't like working in the fields, but preferred walking around the derelict houses, mounds, and mountains. He was a harmless old man. One evening, Hasan visited us and my father asked me also to call Uncle Seyit. After Seyit had arrived, the three of them started a deep conversation. I was preparing tea for them. Hasan took out a few objects from his pocket and started talking about them. I remember that what he said sounded like a joke. I was amused and kept listening. He was saying very interesting things. He said that he needed a few strong men and asked my father and Seyit if they would help him. They said that they would if it was possible. Hasan carried on talking about the mound Salur which was very close to our village. He told them that they were going to go there tomorrow night to dig an area on the west of the mound.

"There are two cauldrons hidden there and one of them is full of gold," he said. "However it isn't easy to take the gold, since there is a guard. Once we start digging, we are going to hear a strange noise, but we are going to ignore it. After a while, the noise is going to increase, but we are still going to ignore it. The owner of the noise is going to appear as a freaky beast, but we aren't going to get scared of it and when we reach the gold, both the noise and the beast are going to disappear."

My father asked what would happen if they couldn't control themselves and freaked out. Hasan said that would be very bad, since they would be thrown away about 70 meters. Following this, my father and Seyit started laughing. Hasan looked at them with anger and asked them why they were laughing so much. As far as he could remember, when he had found Çatalhöyük, they had also laughed at him then. Then what happened?! James Mellaart discovered it and all of them showed respect to Hasan.[2] So "don't enjoy yourselves that much," he said, "because one day, you might need to show more respect to me."

Hasan was right. He is still the most talked-about man in our village for being very clever. Apparently, he would often go to Çatalhöyük, find some beads, and study them. All the fields used to belong to the State in the past and therefore there were no deeds on them. Hasan owned a few fields in the village. When the government officers came to the village to hand the deeds over to the owners, Hasan told them that he didn't want the deeds for his fields, but the deed for Çatalhöyük. His friends laughed at him asking what he was going to do with Çatalhöyük. It wasn't a very prosperous area. He couldn't plant or grow anything.[3] So he would have been crazy to swap his fields for it. Hasan shouted at them with anger saying, "You are crazy, not me! Don't underestimate Çatalhöyük! There is a huge city under that mound!" Nevertheless, he couldn't get the deed for the mound. When he reminded my father and Seyit of this, they both became quiet. Seyit also knew Çatalhöyük well, since he had worked with James Mellaart. So he knew that Hasan had a lot of interest and knowledge about these things, even though he wasn't sure if there was hidden gold on the Salur mound. Hasan would often walk across the old settlements around the village and it was on one such day that he left the village and never came back. Nobody knew what happened to him, and the only memory of him that was left behind was his eccentric life.

5 I build the Çatalhöyük cafe

I was still working at Çatalhöyük as well as doing some trade. I was earning good money. I didn't miss my past as I had a comfortable life without financial difficulties. When I had been working in the city, I couldn't even find the money to put petrol in my car. Now I was driving to the cities near the sea when my shifts as a guard at Çatalhöyük were over. I was also meeting a lot of people. It was getting difficult to find time to spend with my wife and the children. Right after breakfast, I left home for work. My work was intense. My wife said that she missed the days when I used to be a taxi driver. But I was very happy and wished my family to be happy, too. I told myself that although my wife said she was unhappy, they had everything they wanted. What else did I have to do for them? All in all, my life was going very well, and the only people who weren't happy were my wife and the children. I had lived a quiet life before, but now I was doing trade with a friend in the city as well as guarding Çatalhöyük. I was also working in my field, growing beans and wheat. Due to my difficult past, I was always attempting new opportunities. Hence, I decided to open a cafe at Çatalhöyük.

I thought that if I was going to carry on working there, I had to be more helpful for the visitors. There was nowhere to relax and have a drink at Çatalhöyük. Moreover, if the excavation team got bored in the dig house, there was no place to go around the site. Opposite the guard house there was a garden[1] which belonged to the old guard Süleyman. I bought this area and started building a cafe. The visitors who came to Çatalhöyük while I was building the cafe appreciated what I was doing. I was building the cafe using the money I had got when I sold my share of the trade partnership that I had with a friend. The cafe was being built from wood and since this was an expensive material, I also had to use the money I earned from farming. Finally, the cafe was open. We named it Cafe Çatalhöyük. My son and nephew worked at the cafe full time while I was working one week at the site and one week at the cafe. My family was also very happy. I was able to give more attention to my children.

I knew that the cafe wouldn't make enough money, but I was hoping that it would get better. I was wrong. The tourists weren't coming to the cafe. You might think that I was selling things at too high a price. On the contrary, I kept the prices very low. Sometimes, a few people who came by taxi would stop and buy things like water and Coke. However, the tour buses wouldn't buy anything at all.[2] I had opened this place to serve people, but they weren't making use of it. I started focusing on farming again as well as buying and selling cars while my son and nephew were running the cafe. Even though they weren't earning enough money, I decided not to close the cafe down. My biggest problem was that I was not able to sell the stock I had bought. I will give you an example.

It was getting colder and there were a lot of ice creams left in the fridge. There were about 20 men working at Çatalhöyük, all of whom were from Küçükköy. One day, I gathered them together and said that the ice creams were going to be free, but only on one condition. If they bought two ice creams each and if one of all the ice creams had a "free" label on it, they would pay for all the ice creams. However, if none of the ice creams had a "free" label, then all the ice creams would be on me. They were very keen on the idea. I heard some saying "there is no way that there will be a 'free' label on them. So the ice creams will be free!" But what they didn't know was that I was pretty sure that there were at least a few such labels on the ice creams. I was also very happy, since I was going to sell 40 ice creams. After their shift, the workmen came to the cafe and started eating the ice creams. They had eaten 25 ice creams already and still there was no "free" label. I was still hopeful. Except for one person, everybody had taken ice creams and no label had appeared. I was shocked. A friend called Hulusi Yaşlı had kept his ice creams for later. I couldn't believe that I had suffered the financial damage of giving away 40 ice creams free. My only hope was Hulusi and his two ice creams. I was really nervous. I brought Hulusi back to the cafe and asked him to eat the ice creams, but he refused. I must have been very pushy, since in the end he opened one of them. There was no "free" label on it. Hulusi looked at me. I was very quiet. Even though he didn't want to eat it, he started opening the second one. Everybody was watching him. He opened the final ice cream and again no "free" label. All the workmen were very happy. I thought that only an ice cream could extinguish the fire inside me. So I opened one and I couldn't believe my eyes. There was the "free" label. The workmen were laughing at me and saying that I was really lucky. They ate 40 ice creams, but couldn't find the label, whereas the one I picked up had it. I might have lost 40 ice creams, but my luck was equal to it. I said that it was okay and that I hoped they had enjoyed their ice creams. They all went back to work and I was on my own. I want to explain my feelings with a story.

Once upon a time, a shepherd lost his camel and started looking for it. While he was happily looking for his camel, he bumped into two farmers, sitting on the mountain, eating their bread. He asked the farmers if they had seen his camel. They said "no" and added that he did not look upset for a person who had lost his camel. The shepherd said that when he lost his camel last time, he found him grazing on the opposite mountain. So he must be there. But if he wasn't there, then he would get very worried.

I still have a hope about the cafe. If nothing changes soon, then I will be really upset. Hopefully, it will be okay. Then I will see my efforts not being wasted and feel much happier. Until then, I have to carry on working hard and helping the visitors as much as I can.

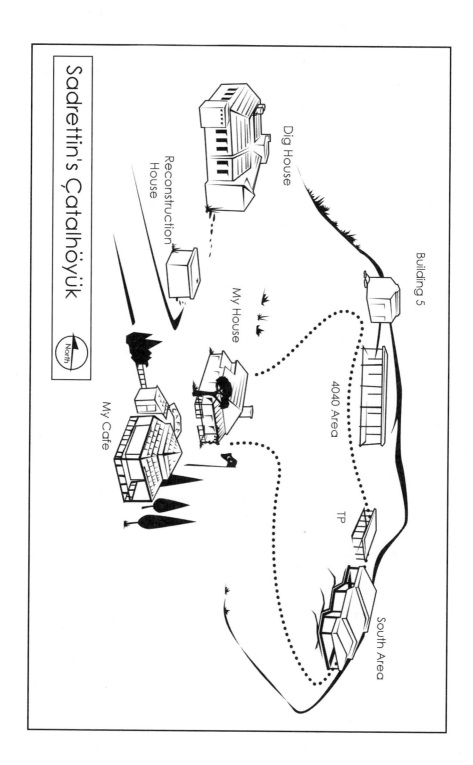

Sadrettin's Çatalhöyük

North

Dig House

Reconstruction House

Building 5

My House

4040 Area

My Cafe

TP

South Area

6 Dealing with more visitors and foreigners

A lot of people who came to our Visitor Center were really enjoying it. I want to talk about one of them. One morning, two visitors arrived at the site. As always, I greeted them at the gate and asked them to wait for me. I was cleaning the Visitor Center. Even though they didn't wait for long, they were being very impatient. When I said that I was ready, their eyes sparkled. One of them was particularly interested. While we were walking around the site, they were listening to me carefully. The very interested one was speaking very politely. I don't know whether it was his manners, speaking style, or his love for Çatalhöyük that made me think that he was a very nice person. After the tour, I asked them if they wanted a cup of tea. They were quite shy. Then I told them that I would have liked to meet them properly. So, we had tea together. I found out that this guy was a solicitor in Konya and his name was Sermet Öten. We had a long chat. I was very happy to meet these people, since they were the kind of people who would have a good influence on me. Therefore when Sermet asked me if I could help him, I was surprised. How could I help an educated guy like him? I felt quite emotional and asked him what I could do for him. He asked me to talk to Ian for him as he wanted to work on the site during the summer. I told him that the work often involved shoveling and emptying soil. He said that it didn't matter as long as he could work at Çatalhöyük. My liking for him increased a thousand times. Whoever likes Çatalhöyük is my best friend, because here is my life source. Anyhow, after we finished our teas, Sermet invited me to his office and they left.

I was on my own again. I was waiting for the next tourists to arrive and getting excited about helping new people. Sometimes, nobody visited the site for days. There were many people who knew about and loved Çatalhöyük, and there were some who didn't know anything about it. Even though I grew up a kilometer from the site, I hadn't known anything about it for many years. So, how will the people who aren't aware of Çatalhöyük get to know about the site? Of course, the excavation director will introduce it to the world. I know that it will take time, but I am prepared to wait and guide people around the site without getting tired. It is all for serving people.

I really like foreign people. Why? During the time that I worked as a taxi driver, I drove trucks for about six months. Once I was collecting fertilizers from a factory with my brother. I loaded the fertilizer on my truck and started driving to Konya. After a while, my brother got hungry and we stopped to eat. It was expensive to eat at the restaurant, so we made our tea in the truck and had some cheese and olives. It was a great view where we stopped. The mountains were sharing all their beauty with us. We ate and continued on our way. By the time we arrived in the Konya region, it was very cold and snowy. I was trying to drive over a hump when the truck stopped and started sliding back. I wanted to jump out of the truck, but I couldn't, since my brother was sleeping. There was a cliff on the other side of the road. If I had jumped out, I could have survived, but I decided not to. If we were going to die, we had to die together. The truck was still sliding back. I was pressing the brake as hard as I could, but it had no effect. We were going to die. I tried one more time before giving up. Suddenly the truck skidded and stopped. My brother woke up. We got out of the truck and realized that the end of the asphalt was sand. The truck had skidded onto the sand, made a pit, and got stuck there. If the truck had moved a meter more, we would have died. I was very happy. It was very cold, windy, and snowy. The truck was leaning toward the cliff. We decided not to get back in it. I was very tired and sleepy. The last town we drove by was about 10 kilometers away. We couldn't walk back that far, so we decided to walk onward. After a kilometer, there was no town or village. I was very cold and tired. I told my brother that I wasn't able to walk anymore and maybe it would be a good idea to go back to the truck. He didn't want to go back. Maybe the truck had fallen down the cliff by now. I stopped him and said that I wanted to think for a minute. If I carried on walking, I was going to freeze and die. If I went back to the truck, it might not be there, but if it was still there, I could survive. I wasn't afraid of death, but I was thinking about my wife and the children. Who would look after them? I told my brother that I was going back to the truck and if I died, he had to take care of my family. My children didn't have to know that I died, so he had to tell them that I was lifted to the sky. There would be a sparkling star on the east and when they looked at this star, I was going to look back at them. He also had to tell them not to worry, because if they got worried, I would get worried more. Anyway, I started walking to the truck. My brother shouted at me that if there was death in the end, we had to die together. So he started walking with me. Neither of us said anything. When we got to the truck, it was still there. I got in even though my brother told me not to. I was very cold and tired. He waited outside for a while, and then he also got in. I laid down. Some noises were coming from the truck. Inside was cold, but we were warming ourselves with a little gas bottle. I must have fallen asleep. My brother woke me up in the morning. When I got out to go to the toilet, I became afraid of the truck which I had spent the night in. The cliff which had looked quite shallow at night was actually about 30 meters high. I got my brother out of the truck. Then we saw a small lorry coming. It stopped. We told the driver what had happened and he took us in his lorry to the nearest town. We found a tow truck and pulled our truck back to the road. Then we went to the town again to have some food with the lorry driver called Ali. He really helped us and therefore we appreciated him. I thanked him and asked how much it would cost. He said to me that if I had been a local, he wouldn't have helped me, since his job was more important than my truck. Because I was a foreigner, he thought that there would be no one else around and he forgot about his job to help us. Apparently, he had experienced a similar thing in the past and couldn't find anybody to help him out. Then he promised himself that if a foreigner got into the same situation, he would help him. So he didn't want any money but asked if we needed anything else. I thanked him again and he left.

I like foreign people the way Ali did. Whatever religion or country they are from, I am always ready to help them. It is nice to like someone and to be liked, but sometimes there is infidelity. You might get hurt by your loved one. How? I want to explain it to you with a joke.

A man gets very ill and tells his wife that he is very scared of dying. He says to her that if Azrail (the angel of death) comes, he would like to ask Azrail not to take his life but to accept his wife's life instead. He asks his wife whether she would be willing to give up her life for him. She says that she couldn't live without him, so her life is his. The man feels very happy thinking that his wife really loves him. But would he do the same thing for her? In any case, he doesn't know whether the answer she gave was truthful, so he asks his son to catch a crow from the garden, to pluck its feathers and to bring it back without anybody seeing. The son completes his duty and brings the crow to his father. The man puts the crow in a cupboard and ties a thread to the handle. When his wife comes, he asks her the same question. Once again she says that her life is his. Then the man pulls the thread and screams saying that Azrail is here. When she sees the crow, she thinks that he is the Azrail and shouts that her husband is the ill one, not her.

Everybody must have experienced the feeling of fear at some point. Sometimes it may occur toward an animal such as a snake. Most people are scared of snakes. In Çatalhöyük, a lot of snakes come out in the spring. I want to tell you a memory which involves some tourists.

It was a nice morning and I was taking five people to the mound. I didn't realize there was a snake on the edge of the path. Suddenly, the people started screaming and running around. I couldn't understand what was happening. Then one of the women (a fat one) jumped on me and before I realized what was happening, I found myself underneath the woman. She was holding my arm so tightly that I couldn't get up. Finally I got up and saw that these people were scared of a snake. I was quite upset, since my manhood had been questioned, especially by a woman. If I killed the snake, I would be appreciated again. So I told them that I was going to kill it. I walked toward the snake with the fat woman by my side. It wasn't big at all. I felt sorry for it. When she asked me to kill it, I said that it wasn't a snake, but a dragon, so I couldn't kill it. One of them sarcastically asked me what kind of dragon it was. I decided not to carry on and told them that I was only joking. It was harmless, so we didn't have to kill it. I have never heard of anybody being killed by a snake either at Çatalhöyük or in the villages. Besides, I couldn't kill anything. I was trying to help all the animals around here as much as I could. I would feed the ants with the flakes from my bread and leave some water for the birds and other animals. There was no reason for them to be scared, so we had to carry on our tour.

I want to tell you another story about snakes. When I was a kid, we didn't have any electricity, so we used to use çıra lamps. This is a lamp with a glass bowl and a long glass cover. Fuel is poured inside the bowl and the lamp is lit by burning a hanging cotton-wool thread. There was no TV or radio, but I wouldn't exchange the long and cozy chats that we had for any of those things. I was told this story by an old lady during one of those long chats. You can decide whether it is true or not! Even though it is hard to believe, I think that it is true. When her grandmother was a child, she found a woolen basket full of baby snakes in the store room. She hung it on the ceiling. The mother snake returned and despite being used to the family, was angry and left poison in the clay bowls. The housewife wondered why the snake was so angry and found that her daughter had put the snake babies in the ceiling. She took the babies down and told the snake to stop making a mess around the house. When the snake was sure that her babies were safe, she went around all the clay bowls and broke them. When the male snake turned up, the housewife complained about what the mother snake had done. They argued and he left. The female snake waited until her babies became adults and then she also left. After this, the family, which used to be very rich, became very poor.

I am very influenced by old stories. As far as I am concerned, the people who lived in old times used to love, help, and joke with each other. However, some of these jokes could be quite offensive. I want to tell you about a joke made by a neighbor of ours called Ahmet Ak. Ahmet moved out of his father's house to live in his own place. He became very good friends with his neighbor Mehmet Ferahkaya. One evening, Ahmet was being chased by a bull. Not able to open his garden gate due to his fear, he jumped over the gate. On the other side of the gate, Mehmet saw him and asked what he was doing jumping over the gate at that time a night. He said that the owner did not want him to wear out the gate, so he jumped over the gate during the night. He did not mention the bull. Then the bull started running toward Mehmet. The bull and Mehmet chased each other for a while. At every turn, Mehmet shouted to Ahmet saying that he would take his revenge. Finally, Mehmet saved himself from the bull and caught Ahmet by his arm, hurting it. Ahmet begged Mehmet to leave him alone, and in the end he did.

7 Some less happy memories

I have always been impressed by how people lived in old times. It may be because I am working at an old settlement. You might wonder if I don't have any bad memories of Çatalhöyük. Of course I have and even though there are only a few, I will share them with you.

One day, Shahina called me, asking whose shift it was. I told her that it was Mustafa's turn. Then she asked if I could help her and I said okay. She said that Ian was going to arrive at Konya airport that evening and he needed to be collected. I did it. Before me, a friend called İsmail, who works in the kitchen, used to collect Ian. He was a good friend of mine. We would always joke with each other. Even after the excavation season ended, he would come to Çatalhöyük to visit me. I would respect him, since he was always ready to help others between all his responsibilities. Shahina asked me to collect Ian a few times. Ian took the excavation team for a dinner in Konya once and they kindly invited me. İsmail was also there. I was happy to see him. I sat next to him together with the museum representative, Osman Ermişler.[1] After they had shaken hands, I attempted to shake İsmail's hand and when I did it, I tickled his hand to show that I was glad to see him. However, İsmail got very pissed off with me. He asked me why I did that as if he was gay. I hadn't intended to imply that; I only wanted to joke with him. I tried to apologize and reminded him that we always used to joke with each other. There must have been some other reason for his anger. I left him and went to talk to other friends, but I found that I had lost all my interest in the night. When we returned to Çatalhöyük, I went home. The next day, I came for my shift and İsmail wasn't talking to me and neither was Osman Ermişler. I wondered why Osman

Ermişler was upset with me. We got on very well, and I didn't think that I had ever done anything to upset him. I was sure that İsmail was responsible. In the evening, Shahina called me and offered me some money. I didn't know what it was for. She said that I had gone to Konya for her six times and she should pay me for that. I said that I didn't want the money, since it was a favor and I would always do it for the team. Shahina said that I needed to take the money, otherwise she would never ask for a favor again. I took the money and went back to the guard house. Osman Ermişler was resting outside. There was a football match on TV, but since he wasn't talking to me, he didn't come into the guard house to watch the match. I approached him and asked if he could come with me to the house, because I needed to talk to him about something. He followed me. I asked him what I had done wrong to upset him. He said that I didn't do anything wrong, but I was making a big mistake by stealing other people's jobs. He wouldn't want to talk to anybody who did that. I asked whose job I was stealing. He told me that İsmail used to go to Konya to collect Ian and now I had stolen his job. I tried to explain the situation by saying that Shahina had sent me to Konya five or six times and that she paid me what I deserved. Even though I tried to say that I had done it as a favor, he didn't accept it. I told him that I didn't know why Shahina sent me to Konya instead of İsmail, but as far as I could see everybody who worked at the excavation house earned some extra money and maybe Shahina thought that I also deserved to make some extra cash. Following my explanation, he agreed with me saying that İsmail had told him a different story. Then I realized that İsmail hadn't actually been offended by my joke, but that he had been looking for a reason to argue against me. If he had talked to me about it, it would have been better. As a result, I found out that money was more important than our friendship. I didn't talk about this to anyone and I want to say no more. I want to finish this memory with a story.

The emperor calls his vezir (assistant). He tells him that whoever brings him an ermiş will be given a bag of gold. Who is an ermiş? He is a person who didn't commit any sins in this world and therefore deserves to go to heaven. The vezir announces this to the public and one man tells him that he can find an ermiş for them, but he has to talk to the emperor first. The emperor summons the man and the man says that he can find an ermiş for him, but first he has to give him the gold and one month of time. The emperor accepts this offer, but tells him that if he can't find the ermiş, he will be beheaded. The man returns home with his bag of gold and tells his wife that the gold should be enough to live on nicely for a month, but does not tell her what has happened. When she says that the gold would be more than enough, he says that she can use it all. As a result, she feeds her husband really well for a month. At the end of the month, the man tells his wife the situation and she cries, but he says not to worry, since they couldn't live their whole life the way they did for the last month. He leaves his family to face his fate. On his way, he sees a person sitting by the road. The person asks where he is going and he says to see the emperor. The person asks to come with him, since he has never seen the emperor. The man tells the stranger that the emperor is going to behead him, so he should not put himself in danger by accompanying him. The person does not listen to him and follows the man. When the man is summoned by the emperor, he admits that he knew that he couldn't find the ermiş, but he and his wife were very poor, so he had wanted to take the gold and look after his family really well for a month. He had to do this as the head of his family. The emperor called his vezirs and asked them what he should do with this man. The first vezir suggested defleshing the man, and the stranger who had accompanied the man said "asleo nesleo." The second vezir suggested beheading him and the stranger said "asleo nesleo." The third vezir said that he was indeed guilty, but that he had admitted his fault. "Being poor is a very difficult thing and he compromised his life for a month's living. Our emperor may behead him if he wants to, but also he may forgive him. What would you lose if a bag of gold was missing from your treasury? I think you should forgive him."

Once again the stranger said "asleo nesleo." Then the emperor asked him what he was trying to say, since he repeated the same words for each option. He said "The first vezir wants to deflesh the man, since his ancestors were fox hunters. The second vezir wants to behead him, since his ancestors were executioners. However, the third vezir asks you to forgive the man like his ancestors would. So, you should keep him and get rid of the other two. You would find the bad people within your state by looking for them, but the good ones are only a car full. And when it comes to me, I am the ermiş that you have been looking for."

Dear readers, it is great that there are a lot of good people in our world. What if there were not?! I will try to tell you with a joke. A farmer fills his car with two buckets of peaches to give to the emperor as a present. During his journey, he can't resist the peaches and he reasons that if he does not eat them, they will get damaged. When he arrives at the palace, he realizes that only one plate of peaches is left for the emperor. He tells the emperor that he ate all the bad peaches while leaving the good ones for him and these were the only ones left. The emperor really likes him and tells his vezir to give him ten gold coins. The farmer is very happy and thinks that if he gives a present to the emperor every year, the gold he gets can make him rich. The following year, the farmer decides to take two buckets of quince to the emperor. On his way, a few zaptiye stop him. What is a zaptiye? This was the name of the policemen during the Ottoman Empire. They ask the farmer where he is going and he says that he is taking some presents for the emperor. They ask what the presents are and he says two buckets of quince. They say that the emperor does not like quince, so it isn't a good idea. The farmer asks what he should be giving to him. They don't say anything. The farmer goes back. The next time he decides to take two buckets of figs, and because he does not like them, he does not eat them. When he arrives at the palace, the emperor remembers him and accepts his present. Once he sees the figs, he gets very upset, since he also does not like figs. He starts throwing the figs at the farmer and every time the farmer gets hit by a fig, he prays. Later on, the vezir tells him that if he had shut up instead of praying, he wouldn't have got beaten so much. Then the farmer replies that he was praying because he felt lucky to be beaten by figs. "What if I had brought quince and he had thrown them at me?"

8 The past and the present

Dear readers, when I think about whether past times or the present time are better to live in, believe me, the past times seem much nicer. Nowadays, technology changes everything very quickly. For instance, nine thousand years ago there was a large lake on the west side of Çatalhöyük and the Neolithic people would benefit from its water, reeds, and fish, as well as the eggs of the birds which would visit the lake.[1] Not long ago, in 1974, our life was also similar to the Neolithic life. There was a canal along-side our village where my friend Osman Güven and I used to fish. One day Osman told me that there were a lot of fish in the canal nearby Çatalhöyük and asked if I wanted to fish there. I said okay. He was right. The canal was full of fish. While we were trying to get the fish inside our netting, a taxi stopped near us. A man and a woman got out of the car and started watching us. We tried not to look at them as we felt embarrassed. The woman was wearing very revealing cloths and it was rude to look at people like that in my village. Besides I had never seen a woman dressed like that before. They were speaking in another language. The only thing that we could understand was the word "Çatalhöyük." I directed them to the site, but they couldn't understand me. Then Osman told me to take them there and come back. I didn't want to because I was scared they would kill me. So I told Osman to take them. He also didn't want to (possibly for the same reason!). Eventually, we decided to take them to Çatalhöyük together. I sat in the front seat. Osman also wanted to sit with me, but the woman stopped him sitting next to me by offering him the back seat. This scared us more. I showed the way to the man and he started driving. When we arrived at Çatalhöyük, we got out of the car and started walking back to the lake. They were trying to tell us something, but we wanted to get away from them as soon as possible. Once we left them, they got into the car again and followed us. We couldn't understand what they were saying. The woman caught Osman by his arm and got him into the car. I attempted to run away, but couldn't. I also got into the car. I told Osman that was it! Obviously, these people had been planning to kill us, since they didn't even visit Çatalhöyük. Osman was mumbling that if he didn't get back home in the evening, his father would kill him. They brought us to where we were fishing and gave some food to us. Being two kids, we couldn't figure out what had happened. We thought that they let us go in the end because they got scared of us. It was good that we didn't show them our fear.

Now we know how nice those people were and we laugh at ourselves. We caught a lot of fish that day. I don't know the situation in Osman's family, but my family needed all that fish, since we were poor. My father would often walk along the canal collecting duck eggs for us to eat. When we were in despair, my father and mother would talk about the past to give us some hope. One day while we were watering the field, we ran out of gasoline. Since we didn't have any money, we couldn't get any more gasoline. My brother and I were very upset. My father called us and asked my mother if she remembered the duck eggs that he used to collect. He talked about more difficult days in the past and started telling a story.

One day, your mother and older sister visited our neighbor's house while they were eating fried eggs. Your sister saw this and when they got back home, she also wanted some eggs. Since we didn't have any eggs, I went to the canal and looked for some duck eggs. I picked up an egg from the first nest that I saw. I smashed it to see if it was okay, but it was stale. Then I looked for another nest in which the eggs were fresh. I collected them and brought them to you, so that you wouldn't be hungry that night. Thanks to Allah that today we have some food to eat. Never give up and always carry on working. I will find the petrol, but believe me that our work is much easier than looking for duck eggs.

After we listened to him, we felt very enthusiastic. He got some gasoline and we went to the field for more work.

It was easier to work in the fields then, since there was always enough water in the canals.[2] Whatever you planted would grow healthily. My brother and I had planted some melon in a field which was quite a distance from our village. It would take a day to bring water to the field from the village. We grew melon there. There was a large grazing area for the animals behind the melon field. We would direct the water to the grazing area in the evenings whereas in the morning, we would water the melon field with the help of a water pump. Nowadays, the situation is difficult. There is not enough water left in the canals or in the wells. This makes the farming very hard. Even 30 years ago, this area was known as a good water source. I am very afraid that if the water problems continue and the State doesn't find a solution, the whole village will disappear as Çatalhöyük did.

As far as I am concerned, 30 years ago life was better than now. Poor people could benefit from nature. Not only was there enough water, but also we would go hunting. We used to hunt duck or rabbit. Whoever went hunting from our village would definitely bring something back. Despite being a kid, I also used to shoot things. It was difficult for me to go hunting as a kid, but I wanted the approval of my mother, brothers, and sisters. One evening, I prepared myself to go hunting the next day. I left home in the morning and started walking along the canals. I got quite far away from the village. The weather was very cold and I was freezing. Since I couldn't find anything to hunt, I didn't want to go back to the village. The previous hunters had frightened all the animals. I considered going back to the village, but they were waiting for me to bring back some animals. I would only go hunting when we desired to eat meat. Although I decided to carry on walking, I was tired and hungry. I kept walking for a little while and then saw a little house which was owned by Nebi who was also from our village. The door was open, so I sneaked in. I collected wood from outside and lit a fire in the fireplace. I was warm and relaxed. After a while I went out, but even though I felt much better, I couldn't encourage myself to carry on. Outside was colder. So I decided to go back to the village. I was quite upset that I was going to return empty-handed. On the way back along the canal, I heard some noises and decided to hide myself. The noises belonged to some geese. I hung onto my rifle and started moving very slowly. In a few seconds I saw the geese flying from the canal. I took my first shot but missed. With the second shot I managed to kill a goose and then another one, even though it was very difficult. I picked up the geese and rushed to the village, because the geese had to be cooked and eaten the same evening. I was very happy.

Dear readers, Çatalhöyük illuminates the life we have lived in the last 30 years. The lifestyle of the Neolithic people was also experienced by the people who have been living around here for many years. Maybe that is the reason I am in love with Çatalhöyük. Now I want to describe the house I live in at the moment to show you how similar it is to a Çatalhöyük house. The walls of my house are made of mud brick. Every three to five years, we collect soil and hay and mix these with water to make mud to apply it onto the walls. Every year, we use white soil to coat the inside walls. We cover the ceiling with long tree trunks and then place straw on top of them. Following that, we coat the top of the straw with clay soil in order to prevent leakage. I also place bricks on top of the clay roof, because otherwise I have to coat the roof with clay soil every year. So, the only difference between my house and a Çatalhöyük house is that my house has windows and doors. Unfortunately nowadays, these houses are slowly disappearing and instead, concrete structures are being built.[3]

9 Dealing with each other

I don't aim to upset you with some of my memories. But there are things that I could never forget and sharing them with you makes me very happy. I am not going to give the real identities of the people who I will be telling about now. They left the village in 1985 to move to the city. I found them and asked permission to mention their names, but they didn't want me to. So I will tell the story by using a fake name. I used to know a girl called Fadime. They were our neighbors. When we were kids, our families used to visit each other very often. In the old days, there weren't many TVs in our village. Since Fadime's parents had a TV, most families would gather in their house. Every Saturday evening, there would be a tear-jerker Turkish movie on. My family as well as the others would look forward to it and everybody would make sure that their tissues were in their pockets. After the movie, nobody would talk to each other and they would secretly carry on crying. How nice those people were! They would cry until the movie ended and the next day they would tell each other about their favorite scenes while they were working in the fields. Before we could get over the movie we had just seen, we would look forward to the next week's movie. Fadime was tall and skinny. She had an ordinary beauty. Because I was older than her, I remember what happened really well. When she became a teenager, she started having concerns about her looks, thinking that she wasn't liked by her friends. She became depressed and distanced herself from everybody. Her problems increased day by day as all her friends started getting married but nobody was interested in her. According to her mother, one of her friends told her that she was very ugly and therefore no one would want her. Apparently, Fadime would often cry in her room and asked help from Allah to make her pretty. Dear friends, I really understand how she felt, because I often feel the same way. I am ugly, too. There is a saying that if you do not like yourself when you look at a mirror, you will die. Nevertheless, whenever I looked at the mirror in the past, I didn't like myself, but I didn't die. The way that I talk is very fast and I can't pronounce the letter "R". When I was a kid, my friends used to tease me. Therefore I tried to speak very fast as I thought nobody would notice my R's then. I always admired people who spoke properly. Unfortunately, some people enjoy criticizing the weaknesses of others and they also must have done this to Fadime. Soon after, Fadime's parents decided to move to the city. Apparently, a guy became interested in Fadime and his parents wanted to marry him to her. Fadime's parents also approved of the marriage. During their engagement period, they got very fond of each other. On the wedding day, the groom and his family came to pick her up in a taxi. While everyone was happily heading toward the registry office, Fadime suddenly felt very ill and died. They took her to the hospital immediately, but it was too late. They got back to Fadime's house and informed her family. Her family was destroyed when they heard the news. I wish that Allah wouldn't give pain like this to anyone. Fadime was a girl who didn't live her childhood, spent her youth unhappily, and once she found someone she loved, she died. I wouldn't describe the people who gave unhappiness to Fadime as nice. She was a lovely person. Even though many years have gone by since her death, her fiancé still remembers and loves her.

A good-willed person shouldn't joke about other people's weaknesses in the same way that an educated person shouldn't criticize others. They say it is better to have one uneducated friend than to have a thousand educated enemies. Everybody makes mistakes, but a good person would face up to the consequences rather than hurting others. I also made mistakes. I want to tell you about one of them. One day, a man and two women came to visit Çatalhöyük. I greeted them at the gate and we started walking toward the mound. On the way, the man picked up a piece of obsidian[1] from the soil and started talking about it to the women. Once he finished talking, I asked him to put back the obsidian where he had picked it up. In a very sarcastic way, he asked me "why"! I told him that there were possibly some other pieces from the same tool around here and if the archaeologists found them, they could complete the whole object. Then he said that we were selling the figurines found on the site anyway. I got very angry. I asked him if I had been the one selling them. He said no, but blamed the previous workers. I told him that he was giving wrong information to his friends and if he was really sure about his accusations, he had to give me the names, so that I could report them to the director of museums[2] and start the investigation. He got very pissed off and started insulting me. I asked him why he didn't complain about it if he was right. They started talking among themselves as I was trying to calm down. They wanted to go around the mound on their own, but I said it was forbidden. The man insulted me again, saying that I had ruined their visit. I said to him to watch his mouth and asked them to leave the mound. I didn't like these people and didn't want to guide them. He kept insulting the other workers on the site. Once again, I asked him to leave. When he saw that I was serious, he said okay, but asked if his friends could stay, since neither had they insulted me nor had they picked up any object. I said okay. After we finished the tour, they left the site. Soon after this, I found out that they complained about me. The director called me to defend myself. I made my defense and got back to work. Now I feel guilty about treating that guy badly, even though I was right. I wish that I had never had this experience. If we can work out how to use our brain, we can live without any trouble. I would like to expand this topic by telling you a short story.

Once upon a time, there was a shepherd. He was always very happy to take his herd grazing and bring them back to the village. One day, the head of the village[3] called him and asked whether he had any problems, since he always seemed happy. The shepherd said that he didn't have any problems. The head asked if he was married. The shepherd said yes and that he loved his wife so much. The head wondered how this was possible, because he himself had three wives and wasn't happy at all. He suggested swapping wives for a month and offered his three wives to the shepherd in exchange for the shepherd's wife. The shepherd accepted the offer. In the evening, the shepherd called the three wives and asked them what their worst habits were. The first one said that she couldn't stop begging. The shepherd showed her a depot and said that she could gather everything that she collected from begging in this depot. The second wife said that she liked seeing other men. He said that she could receive her friends in the house after he left home, but she had to make sure that they were gone before he returned. Finally, the third wife said that she didn't have any bad habits, but she didn't like being a woman. She liked to behave and talk like a man. The shepherd said okay and treated her as if she were a man. The next morning, the head of the village waited for the shepherd as the shepherd left his house looking very happy. The head became very curious and before the month ended, he called the shepherd and asked him how it was that he was still happy living with three wives whom the head wasn't very happy with. The shepherd said that the reason for the headman's unhappiness wasn't related to his wives, but to himself. He had made a mistake by marrying women who weren't compatible with him. When it came to the shepherd, however, he behaved cleverly even though he wasn't compatible with the women. Instead of them tolerating him, he tolerated them and as a result he didn't have any trouble.

People who can be tolerant in this world will always be happy. We all know that we will die one day. Therefore, I advise you to enjoy life as much as you can. Of course, there will be people who don't agree with us on many things, but we should tolerate them. We have to remember that the human population increases through tolerance and understanding. For instance, the Neolithic people who lived thousands of years ago did also get on very well with each other, because, in my opinion, they needed each other. According to Ian, they always helped each other. They didn't have a leader; therefore there was no order. This used to cause many problems within the community. The houses were closely packed together, without streets in between them, so access to houses had to be over roofs and down through an entry in the roof. To get to one's own house required going over the roofs of one's neighbors. The animals also had to climb over or be carried over the roofs,[4] so there was always a risk of an animal falling down. If they wanted to repair their houses, they might damage neighboring houses and this would cause a problem. Ian also mentioned that these people were quite short and skinny.[5] What Ian said made me wonder how they could have had happy lives despite all those complications.

Every evening, I would walk up to the mound, imagining those times and putting myself in those people's places, thinking how I would react to certain situations. Would I tolerate it if my neighbor had damaged my house? I believe that these people were uniting their powers against nature by being nice to each other instead of arguing all the time. In my opinion, their unity increased their chance of survival. Since they were small people, they always needed each other. For instance, when building a house the owners as well as other people would work on it. If there was a danger coming from outside their village, they would all fight against it. I am sure there were also some intolerant people within the community. Ian said that archaeologists studying the skeletons had found that the Çatalhöyük people had fairly comfortable lives. They didn't work too much[6] and only a small number of them migrated to other places.[7] I wonder why some people migrated if there was such a comfortable life at Çatalhöyük. In my opinion, they didn't migrate of their own will, but were driven away. And the reason was their intolerance. They also would not have been driven away by only a few people, but by everyone who lived at Çatalhöyük. If I had lived in those times and if my neighbor's goat fell into my house while passing over my roof, not only would I be nice about it, but I would also apologize and offer my own goat to them, because I would know that if I had become upset about it, the group would have driven me away. Besides, it wouldn't matter if my house got damaged. When my neighbors were repairing their houses, they would also help to build mine. Is it worth throwing away such a nice life for a goat or a house? If I say yes and decide to migrate, then the moving will not be too easy. How am I going to carry my furniture? What is going to happen to my goats? All in all, I would decide that it isn't worth being intolerant of others for the sake of a goat or a mud brick house and the best thing is to be tolerant and understanding. I left the mound feeling happy with these thoughts.

10 Doing the right thing

One day, I was in the cafe writing my book when a friend called Necati Önay asked what I was doing. I told him that I was writing a book. He laughed at me and said that nobody would read my book, since I was nobody. "Professors write books!" he said. I was shocked. He was right. Who was I to write a book? I felt quite depressed and decided not to carry on with my book. However, I needed this book, because I wanted to live. If I became rich and built a school, a hospital, or a hospice, my name would live on after my death. But as I couldn't do this, my only hope was this book of my memories and now this had been taken away by Necati. Meral Atasağun, a friend from the excavation team,[1] saw how upset I was and asked what was wrong. I told her how I felt and she said to me, "Sadrettin, don't give up. You don't have to be a professor to write your book. It is a talent and you have it. There is a famous writer who is a primary school graduate." When she said this, I felt so happy, because I didn't want to die. My book was going to be my life source. I don't know if anybody would read it or if my memories would mean anything to anyone, but I would not be upset with anyone for that. I am just a guard who only went to primary school. I wrote these sentences on 25 October 2003.

Dear reader, I don't know when exactly you are reading this book. Even if you don't read it, I wanted to write it anyway. And if you are reading it, I want you to know that you will be making me alive. I want to thank everyone who is making me alive. I also want to thank Meral Atasağun who encouraged me to finish my book. I am a person who does not forget favors done for me by other people. Only I wish I didn't have bad thoughts! I want to tell you one of my memories which even now I find it difficult to write about.

It was the last working day of the season at Çatalhöyük. There were only six or seven people left who were due to leave the next morning around 4 a.m. to catch their plane at 6 a.m. So it was my last night with these people. Since Ian was also leaving the next day, he had bought presents for both me and my friend Mustafa. I felt very emotional when he gave me my present and I thanked him. Mustafa wasn't there, so Ian gave me his present to pass on to him. After he left, I went back to my house. I was very curious about my present, so I opened it very quickly. It was a bottle of alcohol. I couldn't understand what it was, because the label was written in English. I thought how considerate Ian was and put the bottle in the fridge. Mustafa arrived in the evening and I gave him his present. He opened it and there was a camera! I wished that Ian had bought me a camera, too. When I had finished the bottle, its memory would fade. But with a camera, I could have continued taking pictures of my friends. In the evening, I went to the excavation house to spend the last night with a few friends. I decided to share the bottle with them. When they saw the bottle, they all applauded. One of them asked me where I got it. I told them that Ian had bought it for me. Then they said that it was a very valuable present, so Ian must have liked me so much. I felt terrible at that moment, because I wondered why he didn't buy me a camera, but a bottle of alcohol. What my friends said helped me to see my mistake. We drank a little and everybody went to bed. I went to the excavation house in the morning to say goodbye to my friends. It was painful to think that I was going to be on my own again. I didn't want them to leave.

At Çatalhöyük I never have time to think much during the day. I need to guard the site, guide the tourists. So the time goes by. But when the night arrives, I try to get used to being alone again. The excavation house which was full of noise a few days ago was now very silent. It was like a snake that was ready to hibernate. I was sitting outside, sipping my drink, thinking that there was no one except a fox to talk to about how I felt. The reason for being upset was actually more related to the mixture of feelings in my head rather than to missing the excavation team. I don't want to talk about these feelings, but maybe it is better mentioning the reason that led me to feel that way. One afternoon, my mother, my nephews, and I were sitting outside our house chatting. Suddenly we heard a noise. There was a stork nest in the tree opposite our house. Then I saw a stork falling to the ground. She must have been trying to reach her nest when she hit the electricity wires. I went over to her to see if she was okay. She seemed dead at the beginning, but after I stroked her a little, she started moving. I gave her some water and kept stroking her. After about five minutes, she managed to stand up and started walking toward her nest. But she wasn't able to fly. I followed her at a distance, since I was afraid that the dogs would attack her. She stopped under her nest. I kept an eye on her until she fell to the ground again. Then I ran to help her as she was trying to breathe on the ground. Her babies don't have a clue what is going on, I thought. How could they know that their mother might not be able to come back home? I decided not to go to my home but to look after the stork. It was sunset when the male stork arrived. He was making noises with his beak and I thought he was letting her know that he was home. She wasn't aware of any of it, since she was already dead. Following that evening, I looked after the storks in that nest every day during the week I didn't work. The first morning, I could only find the babies in the nest, and not the father. They were in the full sun—if their mother had been around, she would have protected them from the sun with her body. After a while, the male stork arrived. He had brought some food to feed his babies. Even though life still went on, you could easily sense their unhappiness. Nevertheless I was happy to know that the male stork was strong enough to look after the babies and they got bigger and healthier as the days went by. I wish that Allah wouldn't give pain like this to people and to animals.

One of the skeletons that was found at Çatalhöyük also worried me as much as these storks did. According to Ian, this person's arm got broken during his life, but didn't get treated. So he had to live with a broken arm. I can understand the pain he must have gone through. We are really lucky to live in this century, since I can't imagine how he carried on his life with that pain. Apparently the reason for his death wasn't his arm. I think that he couldn't have managed to hunt or find food in his state and so others must have helped him. Later, I will mention another skeleton that was found in a midden (rubbish) area. This was a person who was excluded from society by being buried outside the walls of a house in the rubbish. So, why wasn't the person with the broken arm excluded? Who were the people helping him? The archaeologists often find more than one skeleton under the houses. So, was there another skeleton found together with this one? If so, are there any family relations between these skeletons? Were there other skeletons with some illness found beneath the same house? If so, the house could have been considered to be a hospital.

In spite of this Neolithic person having a lot of pain, he was lucky to have friends. Humans are lucky to have friends. It is also nice having friends during bad times. I think it would be meaningless to live in this world if we didn't have any. A real friend would be as close to you as your siblings are. These sentences used to be said by older people who also used to tell a story about them. I want to share this story with you. Once upon a time, there was a young guy who spent a lot of money being with his friends and never helped his father. One day, his father said that he wasn't happy with his behavior and was concerned that his son wouldn't be able to look after his siblings after he died. The guy told his father not to worry, since he had many friends to help him. As the days went by, the guy carried on with his irresponsible lifestyle while his father tried to guide him in the right direction. One evening, the father came home with bloody hands, carrying a sack. His family asked what happened and he said that he killed a man during a fight. His son asked what they should do and told his father that he would do anything to help him. The father asked him to take the sack to his friends, to say that he killed the man, and to ask them to hide it. The son went to his best friend first and asked him for help. His best friend didn't want to help him. As he went to his other friends, he received the same reaction. He came back home and told his father that the people who he thought were his friends, weren't the real ones. Then his father asked him to go to one of his own best friends called Ali and to tell him what happened. The son went and found Ali and told him the story. Ali asked him to be quiet, took the sack, and they started digging a hole to hide it. Just then the father came and asked his son to choose his friends really carefully. "Your best friends should be people like Ali. Don't consider everyone who smiles at you as a friend." Then he turned to Ali and said that there was actually a big sheep within the sack. "So enjoy it!"

It is very nice to have a close friend, but I wish there weren't people around who pretend that they are your close friends. Now I want to talk about a friend of mine called Mustafa Tokyasun. He also lives in Küçükköy and we work together at Çatalhöyük. The director of the Konya Museum, Erdoğan Erol, was temporarily sent to another museum and a friend called Yusuf was transferred to the museum instead. After a while Yusuf came to visit the site. I wanted to show him respect as I always had done to my old director. He asked me about the beer bottles that were in a box by the rubbish. I told him that the visitors leave these bottles and we sell them to buy some cleaning products for the site. He told me not to lie, as Mustafa said that I was drinking those beers. I was very pissed off, because even though some of the bottles were mine, some of them were drunk by Mustafa's friends. I felt very intimidated by Yusuf, but I didn't mention Mustafa's friends. If I had told him the truth, he would also have felt intimidated. I realized that even though Mustafa treated me as his friend, when I wasn't around he was trying to backstab me. I really didn't know why he was doing that. "I told you the reason why I collect these bottles," I said to Yusuf. "But if you want to know whether I drink alcohol or not, yes I do and even now I have some bottles in the fridge." He got very angry with me and told me to shut up. When Mustafa arrived, I told him what happened. He apologized about what he had done and I forgave him. We were working together and in the end we were a family. I had to consider him more than myself, so I didn't have any hard feelings for him.

Dear friends, in old times, people would confront their friends. However I forgave Mustafa without finding out what his real purpose was. Make sure you don't forgive people who aren't your real friends. If I hadn't trusted Mustafa as a friend, I wouldn't have gone through pain that I will tell you about later in my book, even though I am a bit afraid of what I will be writing. I never write anything untruthful about anyone. These are my real life memories. I mean to be honest and genuine. If some mistakes were made in the past, I don't want to hide them. So I am not actually afraid of my memories, but of them being misunderstood. I will try to explain with a short story. Two women went to the hamam (Turkish bath). While they were relaxing, one of the women showed the mole on her hip to the other one and said that her husband liked the mole very much and he always said that he loved her when he looked at the mole. The woman asked the other one whether she had the same thing. The other woman said no but asked the first woman if her husband wanted to have sex when he looked at the mole. She said yes. Then the second woman said that the husband probably used the mole as an excuse to have sex with her. That same evening, the woman without the mole told this story to her husband. After a while the two husbands went for a drink. The husband of the woman with the mole decided to leave early. One of his friends asked him to stay, but the husband of the second woman said that he should be let go to look at his wife's mole. They had a fight. Then the husband went home and accused his wife of cheating on him. The happy couple got divorced due to a silly misunderstanding. I wouldn't want my feelings to be misunderstood in this way. My only aim is to share my memories with you. So if I make any mistake, I apologize to everyone.

I try to explain myself clearly in my book, but sometimes I realize that I make funny mistakes. Here is a story about it. Ian and Ayfer Bartu Candan[2] were teaching me English. Ayfer was speaking very good English while Ian was learning Turkish. Ian was telling me about Çatalhöyük in Turkish, so that I could understand and be a better guide for the visitors. When he couldn't remember a word, Ayfer would help him in English. As I was learning more about the Neolithic people, I was becoming more and more curious. One day, Ian was talking about the wall reliefs at Çatalhöyük. These reliefs were very important and it was crucial to understand their meaning. For instance, some houses had rounded parts on their walls which some people thought were a woman's tits.[3] The fact that some vulture beaks were found in these protuberances made them very symbolic. Since Ayfer (who was a woman) was also with us, I got quite embarrassed every time Ian said "tits." If he had said "breasts," I wouldn't have got embarrassed like this. Even though Ayfer started grinning, I kept nodding and Ian did not stop saying "tits." Then he must have realized something, because he made a comment in English. I couldn't understand what he said, but Ayfer said that there was no problem. Ian carried on talking about the tits. After the lesson, I looked in the dictionary and the word was actually written as tits. But in the daily language we often use the word "breast." Everyone speaks funny when they learn a new language. This has also happened to me. Ian made other mistakes like this one.

One day he said to a female worker who worked very hard that she would be very good in bed that night. She got very embarrassed and ran away. However, he didn't mean what he said. When someone gets very tired from work, we say that he or she will like wherever he or she sleeps that night. This is what Ian was trying to say, I suppose, and I think he will realize his mistake when he reads my book.

11 More about Çatalhöyük

I was guarding the site when an old man who lives in Çumra came to visit Çatalhöyük. I greeted him and showed him the information boards[1] before I started the tour. He looked at the boards and said that he didn't need to read them, since he knew a lot about the site. I said okay and led him toward the mound. When we arrived, I could see that he didn't know anything about Çatalhöyük. He looked around and told me that he didn't understand what all the fuss was about. Why were a lot of people coming to see this site? I told him that the archaeological remains which he was looking at were about nine thousand years old and therefore they illuminated our present. When I said this, he asked me sarcastically how they could illuminate the present. I told him that we learned to build mudbrick houses from the Çatalhöyük people. Suddenly, he got pissed off and said that he built his house before seeing Çatalhöyük. As he started walking back, I ran after him asking him to come back, but he said that he had a lot of work to do in the fields, and besides, he saw many demolished houses in his village. I was confused as I realized that the old man was actually right. Many mudbrick houses had been built in my village whereas around Çumra there were many new concrete buildings. So, he couldn't understand the importance of Çatalhöyük for my village, since he didn't come from there.

Nevertheless there are people who love Çatalhöyük. For instance, every year when the excavation team is there, you can see the happiness and excitement on the faces of visitors as they come to visit the site. I want to talk about one of these friends now. I was sitting at the cafe when I saw him and the other guard walking up to the site. As he saw me, he came to the cafe. He looked very excited.

Even though I offered him a drink, he said that he wanted to see the mound, so he didn't have time. It was very interesting to see the two extremes: the old man who didn't like Çatalhöyük and my friend who loves it so much that he doesn't want to waste time having a drink. I really don't know where this love comes from. I want to describe my feelings for Çatalhöyük, but it is very hard. The days are much nicer at Çatalhöyük. We meet a lot of interesting people who come from different parts of the world. Every season, we get together with 80 or 100 people who come to excavate and who try not to argue. Given that Çatalhöyük is a small place where different nationalities, different cultures and lifestyles come together, you might have thought that there would be a lot of arguing. However, we are very content and relaxed with each other. I am very lucky to work in such a place. They say in Turkish that if you are lucky, you will be born as a girl. I guess I am very lucky, since I was born a boy. If I was a woman, they wouldn't hire me as a guard at Çatalhöyük. All in all, I am very happy in my little world. I hope everyone feels the same way about their own life.

As I am talking about the excavation team, I also want to describe our daily life at Çatalhöyük. We start working at 7 a.m. every morning. My house is on the path the team uses to walk up to the site. While I drink my morning tea, I watch them going to work. The interesting thing is they all look very happy in the morning. Normally, people become very moody and stressed when they get up early. But my friends always look happy, both in the mornings and in the evenings. We work until 9:30 a.m. and then have tea break. After half an hour's break, we work until midday and then have lunch. After lunch, we work until 3 p.m. Even though the team doesn't have to work after 3 p.m., I remember seeing some people carry on working for a while. We have dinner at 7 p.m. After dinner, we sit down in the courtyard and chat. Since my English isn't good, I could never completely understand what everybody was saying and this used to upset me a lot. But my friends who knew my situation were always keen to help me improve my English. They would ask me to teach them Turkish while they helped me with my English. However, I got a little worried about this arrangement, since as you know by now, I can't pronounce the letter "R". So, they would teach me perfect English, while they picked up my imperfect Turkish.

As the days went by, what Ian said about Çatalhöyük made me think and I came up with many questions in my head. For instance, he was talking about the other Neolithic settlements in China, Africa, Papua New Guinea, America, Southwest Asia, Turkey, Iran, and Iraq, and how these settlements might be located in certain areas within these countries. He said that despite the fact that these Neolithic settlements developed around the same time,[2] they presented different patterns. Only a small number of people had migrated between some of these places. As I listened to Ian, I started wondering whether all Neolithic people looked like each other. And how much did they migrate? In my opinion they didn't abandon their settlements, but as times changed, they changed their houses.[3] I also think that the Neolithic people who lived in different continents can't have looked alike. I am sure we are the descendents of the Neolithic people who lived in Anatolia in the same way that European people are descendents of the Neolithic people who lived in Europe. Nowadays, human bone studies and the use of DNA testing have significantly increased. It may be quite useful to test the DNA of the Çatalhöyük people and then compare it to our DNA. I think I am ready for this test. If this testing is possible, I could prove that I am a descendent of the Çatalhöyük people. Briefly what I am trying to say is that the Neolithic people stayed where they first settled and they looked different from each other depending on where they settled in the world. Today, the people from the different countries have developed as a result of the Neolithic people who lived on different continents.[4]

If I tell you how my village was founded, you might understand me better. As I learned from the older generation, there was a village called Efe köy near Çatalhöyük. The village took its name from its head man who was called Efe. He had three sons but the oldest and the youngest fell out. The youngest son decided to leave the village, even though the elderly people tried to persuade him to stay. When he was ready to leave the village with his animals and some of his stuff, some other people joined him. After walking some distance, they found a nice area to settle. One day, when the shepherd in the new village was grazing the animals of Efe's son, he saw another shepherd. He wondered who it could be, but soon realized that it was Efe's shepherd who used to be his friend when he lived in Efe köy. They sat down and had a chat. It turned out that Efe's son hadn't actually gone far from the village, even though he thought that he had. When the lake between his and his father's village dried out, both villages saw that they were quite close to each other. After the shepherds met, Efe took his oldest son with him to visit his youngest. The two brothers made up. Then Efe asked his youngest son to return to his old village. The youngest son didn't want to go back and said that he had founded his village here with people who trusted him. So, he wanted to stay in his village with his people. This was how my village, Küçükköy, was founded.[5]

12 Some erotic moments

I want to go back to talking about the days of the excavation team. The evenings are really nice at Çatalhöyük. Especially the Thursday evenings. . . . Since Friday is the day off, we gather together on Thursday evenings, sitting by the fire, drinking our beers and dancing. The next day some of the team stay at the excavation house, while others go to Konya for a day trip. I always had a great time with these people and never wanted them to leave. Therefore I tried to be with them as much as I could before they left. I was also impressed by some of them. For instance, one of my friends would always read a book in tea break during the work week. I would have thought that he would be tired, just wanting to drink some tea and relax, but no. He would read his book as if someone was going to take it from him. I also want to mention something about our director, Ian Hodder. One morning, I was sitting outside my house when Ian was coming down the mound. He was collecting the rubbish he saw along his way. He greeted me, threw the rubbish away, and carried on his way. I felt respect for him since he was contributing to keeping our environment clean even though he was our professor. I walk on the same path almost every day, but I have never collected the rubbish. I thought that it wasn't my job. As a result of Ian's behavior, I realized my ignorance and started collecting the rubbish. But then my behavior affected Ian, since there was no rubbish left for him to pick up. I was doing some cleaning on the site anyway, but it wouldn't be every day. Now, whenever I go up to the site, I collect the rubbish. This made my work easier, so that I didn't have to go up to the mound during the cleaning hours.[1]

While I am talking about cleaning, I want to tell you about another memory. As I mentioned previously, the museum director Erdoğan Erol was transferred to a different museum. One day, I heard that he was back. So I immediately called my wife, asking her to come and clean my guard house. The house was actually clean, but I knew that Erdoğan Erol was very picky. My wife arrived in the evening and we cleaned the house. After she left, I went to the excavation house. The government representative asked me why I looked very happy. I said that Erdoğan Erol was back and he would possibly come to the site tomorrow. As I expected, he visited us the next day. I greeted him and invited him into my house. He looked around very carefully before we went outside. Then he saw a spider's web on the wall and looked at me without saying anything. I told him that I had cleaned the house the day before, but the spiders must have made another web. I don't know if he believed me or not, but he carried on walking. I was so happy that he had returned. It is very hard for me to describe my feelings, since I am a person who can't express his feelings to others. I have always been the same. I believe that we should enjoy life as much as we can without worrying too much about ourselves. It is up to us to make the world livable.

Though it is a little erotic, I want to tell you one of my memories related to this thought. When I was younger, I had a friend who lived in the city[2] because of his father's job. I thought that he had more experience than me and so I always listened carefully to what he said about things. One day, I asked him if he had a girlfriend. He said yes and carried on, "Sadrettin, city life is different. You have to keep your woman happy all the time. Otherwise, she will leave you." I asked him how to do that. He started telling me how to treat a woman during sex. I don't want to give details of what he said but he told me what to do while making love to a woman and what the signs were when a woman wanted sex. I learned a lot from him. After a while, I also had a girlfriend. Even though I applied everything that I had learned from my friend, I couldn't see the signs that I expected. Obviously, I was doing something wrong. So I asked her if she felt anything. She said that she was feeling things. I asked her what exactly she felt. Apparently she felt ticklish. I stopped and asked her if she was a villager. She said that she came from the city. I thought that there was either something wrong with me, with my friend, or with this girl. Months later, I told this to my friend and he said that he had teased me. I didn't get upset with him, because friends always joke with each other. I just thought that I should not have been so naïve. I realized that my girlfriend wasn't the one who was a villager, but I was. I like being naïve, though, because I know that if someone plays a joke on me, it isn't that I am stupid or not educated enough to get the joke, but that I am too nice to think that it is a joke. Anyway, whatever happens, life goes on.

One day, I was guiding someone around the site. Not only was he listening to me very carefully, but he also seemed to be really enjoying it. After we finished the tour, he asked me about my education. I told him that I graduated from primary school. He was shocked. He thought that I had a higher education, since I knew everything about the site. I told him that at the end of every season, Ian Hodder took me and the other guards around the site and told us about Çatalhöyük. Then we passed this information on to the visitors. He said that he really appreciated the information I gave him, but he didn't think that the site itself reflected what was known about it. I think he was right. If we could reconstruct a few more experimental houses and create a fake mound over them, Çatalhöyük might be more understandable for the tourists. Moreover, it would be good to build a parking lot for the tour buses, since they always have difficulty getting in and out of the site.[3] I also think that the number of toilets in the museum should be increased. In the past, the amount of tourists who visited Çatalhöyük was very low. Nowadays, this amount is significantly increasing and I am sure the visitors would very much appreciate any improvements to the site.[4]

As I was writing these sentences, I was distracted by a TV commercial. It was advertising one of those erotic phone numbers. Out of curiosity and a little boredom, I called the number. Initially, I didn't understand what this woman called Dilerya was talking about. It was actually very embarrassing. But later, I started talking to her about more serious things and we had a normal conversation. I realized that the job one does may not reflect one's real personality. I asked her whether she would give up her coat if she saw a poor person cold on the street. She said that she would, as well as give him half her money. I was very surprised, wondering how a nice girl like her could work on erotic phone lines. It is true that whatever our job, we should be understanding and tolerant, but not ignorant. Ignorance has nothing to do with education.

13 Financial dealings

Educated people can be ignorant sometimes. When I was a kid, my brother bought a watering system from his friend. Since we couldn't pay for it in one go, we paid for the first half and negotiated to pay the second installment in three months. After two weeks, a solicitor called and wanted us to pay our debt. We were very upset since we had agreed on extra time to pay the second half of the money. The only thing to do was to sell our cow. If we were rich, selling a cow wouldn't hurt us. However, it was the only cow we had. If we sold it, what would we eat? If my brother's friend had waited three months, we could have paid our debt without selling our cow. Finally, my father sold the cow. When we brought the money to the solicitor, he wanted more than we initially discussed. Even though we argued, there was nothing that could be done because we hadn't asked for a written agreement when we paid the first installment. My father gave what money we had and asked for more time for the rest. I wanted to object to this situation, but my father said that some people are cruel. The lesson here is that we should not buy anything in installments. If we do, then we have to make sure that we choose the right people. Even though my father didn't want to argue anymore, I decided to fight for our rights and look for another solicitor.

There was a man sitting in the solicitor's office. I thought he was the solicitor, but he turned out not to be. He asked me to wait and I started thinking about how to pay the solicitor. I asked his assistant how much the solicitor would charge just for a consultation. He told me the fee and said that if he decided to work on the case, he would discuss the charge. I said okay and carried on waiting for the solicitor. He arrived and I told him about my situation. He said that I was in the right and that he would help me. As I was about to leave the office to call my brother, the solicitor slapped me on the face saying that I should have paid the consultation fee. I was shocked since I had thought I would come back and discuss the fee. I muttered that I intended to pay his fee. When I asked how much it was, he told me a price different from that indicated by his assistant. I didn't have that much money. So I told him that my money wasn't enough for the consultation. He seemed very pissed off, but said it was okay. I left his office feeling terrible. When I went to see my brother, he asked me why I looked so upset. I didn't say anything to anyone and decided that my father was right. If you didn't have any money, you didn't have rights.

This situation must have upset me so much that even now I am afraid that I will be rejected by whomever I shake hands with. For instance when I go to an official place, I always feel uncomfortable and intimidated. Thanks to Allah, I earn good money now. I have left the bad times in the past. Obviously, I am not rich, but I earn better than when I used to be a taxi driver. I don't complain about anything. The only thing I want is everyone's happiness. I feel very upset when I see people unhappy. Sometimes, it is also very hard to understand why some people are happy and some aren't.

One day, three people came to visit Çatalhöyük. After we finished the tour, the tour guide asked me if they could have breakfast on the table which was outside my house. I said of course and cleaned the table. They asked me to join them, but I said that I had already had my breakfast. As I was making tea for them, they started their breakfast: some bread, tomato, cheese, and olives. The older person was eating as if he had not eaten for two days. I felt sorry for him. I didn't know where he came from, but I thought that he was poor. If he wasn't, he wouldn't eat in my house. I wondered what he was doing for a living and why he traveled all the way here. It is hard for a poor person to travel. I know that from my own experience. I really wanted to help him. As these thoughts were running through my head, the tour guide called me. He said that the man wanted to know why I had been watching him so carefully. Was there a problem? I said that there was no problem, but I felt very sorry for him. He had traveled all this way without any money. I wished that I had been paid, so that I could help him a little. When the guide translated what I had said, the older man started to laugh. I panicked and asked the guide if I had said anything wrong. Apparently, the man was very rich and really liked the fact that I felt sorry for him and thought that he was poor. I was very happy to find out that he was rich. Now I know that people may look different from what they are; but when I see them upset, I still feel upset, too.

Even though I love being with people, I always try to avoid it. The reason is that I cannot speak properly and so feel that people will make fun of me. But I think the most important reason is that my father was poor when I was a kid. You might wonder what this has got to do with my shyness. I will tell you. When I was a kid, I set up a barana with my friends. What is barana? It is five or six people getting together every evening in each other's houses, drinking tea and chatting. One evening, while we were in our friend Ali Kayserili's house, other friends called Alpaslan Tat and Yakup Ferahkaya were joking with each other by criticizing each other's tractors. Alpaslan was saying that his tractor would tow Yakup's in any circumstance. Yakup became very angry. Even though his tractor was smaller, it was a famous make and more expensive and reliable than Alpaslan's. As I saw Yakup getting angry, I wanted to defend him. However, Yakup didn't let me speak, saying that I didn't have the right to speak, because I didn't even own a tractor. I shut up as there was no need to carry on. I will tell you now what I wanted to say to Yakup then. I was going to say that in spite of his tractor being small, if he had sold it, he could have bought three tractors like Alpaslan's. After that evening, I never attended any more baranas. Not even today! We were all kids and anything that we had belonged to our fathers. If my father was poor, was it my fault? My only fault was to have a poor father. I was very proud then. When my brother went to do his national service, he sent us a letter asking for some money. Since it wasn't the farming season, we didn't have any money to send him. Finally my father found a menial job. He was going to look after some bulls. When I found out about it, I got very upset and told my mother that I didn't want him to do this job. What would my friends think of this? Were we that desperate? She told me that it wasn't shameful to work and my father needed this job to be able to send money to my brother. One day, I saw the stable door open and assumed that my father had gone to look for the bulls. He must have left the door open in case I found them first. So while my father was hoping for my help, I was still arguing with my mother saying that he should not do this job. I felt very guilty and decided to help my father find the bulls. I managed to put the bulls inside the stable before my father. When my father arrived, I told him that the bulls were already in the stable. He thanked me and stroked my head. I told him that from now on I was going to be in charge of the bulls, so he didn't have to work. The next day, he sent the money he had earned to my brother.

One day, a friend of my father called Bayram Büyüktemiz came to visit us. We knew that he wanted to help us. The way he was talking was very nice, making us feel that he wasn't actually helping us, but asking for help from us. He asked my father's permission for me to work with him in his fields. In exchange, he was going to send his water pump to our fields. My father accepted this offer and we were very happy. In the evening we went to Bayram's house to talk about the details. We were sitting on the balcony. My friend Ahmet was also there. I had just had a bath and Ahmet had just woken up. We were very cold. Bayram and my father were chatting. Bayram was saying that as long as the children were around, the families could do any kind of work. When I heard that I started laughing. Everyone was looking at me. My father asked me why I was laughing, but I couldn't explain because I was laughing so much, and he became very angry. Ahmet asked me why I was laughing. I told him that his father had hopes for us young, energetic people, but we were so cold. I didn't know whether we would help them or they would help us. When I said this, Ahmet also started laughing.

Bayram was a great man as he didn't only help us, but everyone in the village. One day when I was still working for him, he heard that we had sold our cow. He came to visit us. Apparently, he wanted to give us a cow. He had five or six cows and he gave us the best one. His way of offering it to my father was also interesting. He told him that he didn't like one of his cows because it was always running away. Therefore he wanted to sell it to my father for a good price. During the night, they kept telling old stories and memories. Bayram insisted my father tell the donkey story. Finally, my father gave in.

> When I was a kid, I was coming back from the field on a donkey. I saw an old woman sitting under a tree and crying. I asked her why she was crying. She said that three of them had set out for the village. Two of them had donkeys, but she didn't have one. The other two had told her that she could put her bags on their donkeys and she could walk. She said okay. When they had arrived in the village, she was bitten by a dog. It was so painful that she couldn't walk any longer. Her friends had told her that she was slowing them down, so they needed to leave her there. She was worried that her children would be hungry and would be wondering where she was. I couldn't stand her crying and told her to wait for me. I went back to my house and without

telling anyone, took some flour, cheese, and butter to give to the old woman. I also gave her the donkey, thinking that she couldn't walk in her state. When I returned home, my mother asked me where the donkey was. I said that he was grazing in the garden. Later mother decided to bring the donkey in before the evening. After a while, she came back and said that the donkey wasn't there. I said that maybe it had run away. My mother went to look for the donkey in the village. I couldn't tell the truth, because I was very afraid of my mother. She couldn't find the donkey in the end and I said that thieves might have stolen him.

After this story, Bayram and his family left. The next morning, I went to work. My father came after two hours. My father and Bayram bargained over the cow. I have never seen such a thing before. Bayram was saying that the cow was 60.000 TL[1] while my father was insisting that it was worth 80.000 TL. Bayram was arguing that the cow was very naughty, but my father was saying that he was selling it for too little. When Bayram's brother arrived, they asked him about the price. Bayram said that even his brother agreed on 60.000 TL, so why did my father want to give more money. My father said that he wasn't actually offering more money, but was offering what the cow was worth. Finally Bayram said that he had decided not to sell it for either price. Instead, he divided the difference into half. I was so happy. We didn't have any milk, any food, or any cheese. We got the cow. After a while, we noticed that the cow didn't have any bad habits. On the contrary, it was very tame. So it was clear that Bayram had sold it to us for our benefit. We paid for it when we sold our wheat. I worked with Bayram for three or four years. I also got along well with his son Ahmet. He was a very nice boy. Even though I was working for them, they never treated me like a worker. I was like their son. I can never forget what they did for me. Nowadays, we live in better conditions. The most important thing is I love my job. I do it not because I need it, but because I love it with all my heart. If I describe now a friend who offered me a job, I am sure that I can provide a better explanation of my love for Çatalhöyük.

14 More visitors to Çatalhöyük and some difficult moments

It was a hot summer's day and I was guiding tourists around the site. A taxi stopped outside my house. Two people got out of the car, one of them calling me to ask if they could join the group. I asked the tourists if this was okay and they said it was fine. When they arrived, I saw that one of them was a close friend of mine called Mehmet Akbulut. He had a friend with him called Kazım. After touring the site, we went back to my house to have some tea. Kazım seemed very interested in Çatalhöyük. It was very nice to have a chat with both of them. After the tea, Kazım asked if we could go back to the mound again. So we went up and I was talking about the site while they were listening very carefully. Kazım was asking me a lot of questions. It was clear that he was well impressed by Çatalhöyük. When we finished, Kazım said to me that he could find me a more comfortable and better paid job. I told him that I was very happy with my job and that even if I was fired, I wouldn't leave here. I would sit by the entrance and guard the site without taking any money. They really liked my attitude and left, but they thought that I was very lonely and bored.

However, I wasn't lonely as I had cats. My older cat understood me better than the others. When I was on my own, I would start shouting. My cat would think that I was angry and start watching me until I scared him off. After two or three hours, he would start meowing at me and as I would say sweet things to him, he would come over to me. At night, when he would sleep on his cushion, I would start shouting again. He would look at me knowing that I was upset and he would come to tickle me. He was a lucky cat, since he could always eat what he liked. A female friend from the excavation team also had a cat on the site.

One day, she brought some canned fish for the cats and told me to feed them with a few fish every day. My cat and her cat were sharing the fish as well as the food that I was feeding my cat. My shift was over and it was Mustafa's turn. I gave the canned fish to Mustafa and told him to feed the cats every day. When I came to the site after two days, I saw Mustafa eating the fish. The cats were around him, meowing like crazy. I told him to give the fish to the cats. He ignored them saying that he didn't care about other people's cats. Wasn't he as worthy as these cats? I didn't want to carry on talking to him. I think that the female friend also saw this situation, and she has never brought fish again. But I never left the cats hungry.

One day, I didn't realize that my cat was sleeping under my car and I ran over him. I was terribly upset. I can't explain my feelings. It was going to be very difficult to live without him. I wished that I had never got angry with him. Even though I could have got another cat, I knew that it would never take the place of my older cat. Besides, I wasn't emotionally ready for looking after another animal. Nevertheless, there were a lot of animals living around my house and they all needed my attention. For instance, the birds needed to be given water twice a day while the ants needed some bread crumbs. It was always nice to look after them as they were sharing my loneliness. One evening, my son told me that he had seen four puppies on his way from the cafe. I went to have a look at them. They looked healthy, but very hungry. They needed some attention. I considered taking them home with me, but this would have been very difficult, since they were going to become huge dogs in six months' time. I decided that the best thing was to look after them where they were. I went back home. My wife gave me some bread and said that we couldn't feed them with bread every day, because we were running out of flour. She was right; however, she didn't know how desperate these dogs were. I told her that we had to look after them even if we stayed hungry. When I got back to the dogs, they were waiting for me. Some of them ran away, since they weren't used to me yet. As I gave out the bread, all the puppies turned up and started eating. While they were eating, I went over to the cafe to bring them some water. In the meantime, I was thinking about the owner of the dogs. Such a cruel person! Their mother had helped and guarded the owner all this time, but when she gave birth, "You threw these puppies out. Would you do it to your own children?" As these thoughts were running through my head, I arrived home. The next day, my son took some bread for the pups. He had made some money at the cafe the same day, so we bought two sacks of flour, one for us, one for the puppies. We took bread to the puppies every day. When they got a little bigger, some people adopted them. Two of the dogs followed us to the cafe and they started eating the leftovers from the visitors. They were very healthy and happy. When the cafe was closed during the winter, they stayed in Çatalhöyük. After a while, they were also adopted by people as guard dogs.

In spite of being happy working at Çatalhöyük, I also had bad times. It was a very windy night. I was watching TV in my house when I heard a voice. I turned off the TV and started listening to it. Even though the wind was very noisy, I could distinguish a male human voice, coming from a distance. It was hard to hear what he was saying. As far as I could understand, he was shouting, "Where are you? Help me!" I wasn't afraid. I left the house and tried to figure out where the voice was coming from. Suddenly I realized that the voice hadn't got louder when I went outside. Now I was scared, because I knew that it wasn't a human voice. I went back to my house and the voice stopped. I opened the curtains and watched the gate which was lit by the road lights. I covered myself with a blanket and started listening to the voice very quietly. It came on and off. My room was very quiet and I could hear the clock ticking. It was annoying me, so I put it in the other room. I was trying to concentrate on the voice. Sometimes it sounded like a human voice, sometimes like a tree. I couldn't sleep at all. It was 2:30 a.m. when it started raining. The wind had calmed down. I felt relieved, since the voice had also stopped. I was watching the rain from my bed.

Just as I was feeling okay, I heard an explosion at the dig house. Then the electricity went off. Everywhere was dark. The only light was coming from the road lights, since they weren't connected to the same electricity line as the dig house. I knew that I had to go and check the dig house. I was wondering who could have cut the electricity. It had to be a human because the evil wouldn't do it. If it was a human, then why was I so scared? I was very confused and worried about checking the dig house. I could just pretend that I hadn't heard anything, but this would mean that I didn't care enough about Çatalhöyük. Even if nobody knew, I loved Çatalhöyük very much. And whatever I did for it, I would do it because of my love, not because I wanted to prove something to someone. So the most important thing was to prove my love for Çatalhöyük. I wore my coat and took a stick with me as I walked to the dig house. First, I checked the depot.[1] It was okay. As I was walking around the house, I saw that there was fire in the electricity box. I turned off the electricity switch. Thank goodness I had gone to have a look, since there might have been a big fire. The thunder and lightening must have hit the electricity box. I came back to my house and stayed awake until morning. To be honest I felt very good, since I hadn't been defeated by my fear and I had done my duty. I felt much better in the morning, but was feeling tired due to the events of the previous night. It was one of the longest nights that I spent on the site. I wouldn't like to experience anything like that again.

I was very scared that night and events had happened that were out of my control. Nevertheless some people like to create fears for themselves. I know someone like that, but I won't reveal his name. If I do, he might get offended.

The event that I want to tell you about is very interesting and it happened at Çatalhöyük. I want to let the visitors know that there is a grave on the east side of the mound which belongs to a woman called Güllü.[2] I want to talk about her burial. This woman often came to the village to chat up men and one day she died while drinking and having inappropriate fun. Villagers decided to bury her at Çatalhöyük, since their aim was to make Çatalhöyük the village cemetery. After the first burial, James Mellaart discovered Çatalhöyük and saved it from being a cemetery. However, Güllü's grave was left untouched. Apparently, she had gold teeth, but nobody tried to steal them because she was a foreigner.

One day, two men called Rafan and Kara started digging Güllü's grave to steal her teeth. Since the body had been buried recently, they reached it in a very short time. As they were trying to pull the teeth out, Güllü screamed. One of the men got very scared and ran away. When he arrived at the village, people tried to find out what had happened, but he couldn't speak. After a while, he told everyone what had happened. The villagers went to Güllü's grave to rebury her and told the man that she couldn't have shouted, because she was dead. The only thing that might have happened was that some air left within the body might have come out when they put pressure on it, making a noise. The man insisted that she screamed.

When it comes to me, I am not sure whether the voice I heard that night belonged to a human or not. We sometimes experience things like this, then we remember them with either a smile or hatred. I really don't like thinking about this particular memory. But I always like to remember the memory which I am about to tell you. I found out that there was a river about 100 km away from Çatalhöyük. I was thinking of setting up a fish farm to increase my work options so I decided to drive there to explore the area. My friend Mehmet Eken told me that his father owned a cafe in a village close by and also one of the shepherds would help me if I needed anything. So I didn't have any worries. I followed the route that Mehmet described and I arrived at the village. The shepherd who was supposed to help me was waiting. Both of us got into my car and I started driving on a very stony road. After a while, the shepherd told me that the road didn't carry on, so we had to walk. We had a good chat on the way to the river. After walking 2–3 km, we arrived at a little house which was surrounded with a wire. Apparently, it was the shepherd's house. He said that after he had made sure that the animals were within the wired field, he would relax in the house. To be honest, I envied him, because his house was situated between two mountains, looking at a forest. It would be such a quiet and nice place to live, I thought. After we sat down and had tea, I told him that I was late, so I wanted to see the river quickly. When we got to the river, I was a little surprised. The water which was running between the rocks created very sweet scenery, but the area was too small for what I was planning. "I was looking for a larger area," I said to the shepherd. He looked sad and asked me if I wanted to leave or to have some food with him. I told him that I was late, so I had to leave. He offered to walk me to my car, but I thanked him and told him to go back to his flock. As I started walking toward my car, I noticed how beautiful the mountains were. It was very quiet and I felt so happy.

However my happiness didn't last long. When I reached my car, I saw that the front tire was flat. I felt like laughing. I changed the tire, but as I did so the car slipped down the side of the hill. I tried to rescue it on my own, but it wasn't possible. So I decided to ask for help from my shepherd friend. It was getting darker. I walked toward the little house. When I arrived I shouted, but there was nobody around. The flock also wasn't there. I decided to wait until he returned. The house door was open. I went inside and lit the gas lamp. I was hungry, so I made some tea and ate some cheese, tomato, and bread. While I was waiting to drink the tea, I must have fallen asleep. When I woke up, it was 11 p.m. The tea was cold, so I reheated it. I went outside. It was very dark. I was a little afraid.

I could hear the dogs barking and the sheep bells ringing. I saw the stars shining in the sky. They felt so close to me. Then I started thinking about our planet, the moon, and the northern star. I wondered if there was another planet like ours which is full of people. In my opinion, there must be, since there are such a lot of stars that some of them must have people. I wanted to choose a star for myself. It was going to be mine, but no one else's. Maybe the star I chose would have people on it. Then I would have a lot of friends. While these thoughts were going through my head, I wondered if those people that lived on other stars would also think about us. Would we be able to communicate with our instincts? As you know, our instincts have an incredible power. For instance, humans can't estimate when an earthquake will happen, but animals can. I witnessed it. One afternoon, my cat suddenly woke up and started running around like crazy. I couldn't understand what had happened to him. Then the earthquake happened.

I tried talking to my instincts as I chose a star for myself. Now I was richer, because I had a star as big as our planet. I know this is a bit childish, but there was a song when I was a kid. It went something like this: "There is a village far away and it is our village. Even though we can't go there, it is still our village." I adapted it to my star, saying that there is a star far away and it is my star. Even though I can't go there, it is still my star. After a while, I went inside the house. I was still on my own and started wondering how long I would have to wait. What if nobody turned up? I decided that even if the shepherd came soon, I couldn't leave at that time of night. So the best thing to do was to sleep. I woke up at 7:30 a.m. and realized that nobody had come. I didn't want to wait anymore, so I left the house and started walking to my car. As I passed a hill, I saw the shepherd and his flock. I went up to him but realized he wasn't the shepherd I knew, but someone else. I told him what had happened. He told me that I wasted my time waiting for them since they spent much of their time on the mountains during the summer. He kindly said that he would help me anyway.

We arrived at my car. In spite of trying hard, we couldn't lift it. We walked to the forest and got a fallen tree trunk and used this as a lever to lift the car. I thanked him and told him to say goodbye to the other shepherd. Since the road was very bad, I drove very carefully. I was afraid that the tire would deflate again. Anyway, I managed to get home safely. But I was sad that the water source was quite small. I guess my idea wasn't supposed to happen. Luckily, we had what we needed both financially and emotionally. I hadn't forgotten the days when I worked as a taxi driver. Thanks to Allah, I had a nice life for the moment. The most important thing was not to change as a person. If I made a mistake, my friends might think that the money had changed me. I never wanted to change, and my friends were very important for me. However, some of my friends considered me a bad person without really understanding me. I want to tell you a memory about this.

One day, one of my friends called Mevlüt Ürün called and asked me to get ready to go to the beach. Although I had work to do, I agreed. We arrived at the beach around 3 p.m. Mevlüt was well prepared and had brought his swimsuit with him. I didn't have a swimsuit, but my underwear was clean, so I thought that I could swim in it. When I was in the sea, however, I realized that my wet underwear now revealed everything. I decided to wait for everyone to leave before I got out of the sea. Unfortunately, the beach was never empty. Some people were leaving while others were arriving. Mevlüt called me, saying that he was hungry. After a while, I couldn't wait anymore and came out of the sea. I wished I had not done it, because everybody started applauding me. I felt very embarrassed and quickly got dressed. After the meal, we went to visit my brother-in-law Mehmet Özköylü who worked as an interpreter in a tourist hotel. We had a nice chat and then Mehmet asked if we wanted to go to the hotel beach. Mevlüt started laughing. I didn't want to go, because I didn't have a swimsuit. I told Mehmet what had happened and that I needed to buy a swimsuit first. Mehmet told me that he had a lot of swimsuits, and I could use one of them. He brought me one and we went to the beach, waiting for Mehmet to finish work. When I went to get changed, I saw that my swimsuit was different from the other guys'. Apparently it was very expensive, but I thought that it was also very embarrassing, since it was tiny and therefore looked very sexy. There was nothing I could do. I had either to wear it or get another one from the market. I decided to ask Mevlüt's opinion. He told me that my swimsuit was very nice and that if I didn't like it, he would swap his with mine. I didn't accept his suggestion. People looked at me every now and then, but then I thought that everybody would look at a nice swimsuit. I thought that expensive swimsuits should look sexy. Later on, we went to a cafe with Mehmet and after two or three hours we went to some other beaches. We traveled around for four days. When I got back home, I found out that my swimsuit was a very good make. Since then, every time I go to the sea, I wear it. Its sexiness doesn't bother me anymore. I will keep it for the sake of the old days, even if it gets worn out.

15 They stroke the soil with love

To be honest, I only made this trip to make my friend happy. I didn't regret it, though, and I must have needed a holiday. Anyway, after the beach holiday I got back to my work at Çatalhöyük. Since I loved my job, every time I started a new week, I would feel as excited as my first day. I went up to the mound to see the excavation team. It was very hot. They were inside the tent[1] as usual, excavating and drawing. Even though it was hotter inside, the team was working as hard as ever. I sat down and started watching them. They all looked very hot and sweaty, but no one was complaining. Normally, when we are hot, we feel very frustrated. But these people looked very happy as well as excited. I really can't understand where this enthusiasm comes from. I think while they excavate they go back nine thousand years ago and don't feel the hot weather. I wish I knew what goes through their minds while excavating. As far as I can observe, they think about nice things, because it seems like they stroke the soil with love rather than just excavating.

At this point, I want to continue with a joke relevant to this. A guy carries his mother around for seven years in order to gain her love and respect. One day, he bumps into an elderly relative. His relative asks what they are doing around here. The guy says that he has carried his mother around with him for the last seven years to gain her love and respect, but that he doesn't think he has achieved what he wanted yet. The relative asks him if he has ever asked his mother whether she wanted a husband. When the guy says that she is too old to want a husband, his mother slaps his head saying that he doesn't know better than his older relative.

So, all in all, I should not talk too much. Would I know better than the excavation team? I don't think so. My duty is to guard the site and help them as much as possible. While I was thinking about these things, the female government representative (temsilci) came to visit me one morning. I was about to have breakfast when she told me that she was going to do some aerobics and I could join her if I wanted to. I thought that maybe she didn't like to exercise on her own, so I decided to keep her company. I sat down and started watching as she asked me to join her. I said that I didn't know how to do aerobics even though I really wanted to exercise. A lot of people from the excavation team go jogging in the afternoons. I also wanted to run, but it wouldn't be right to leave the site. So it seemed that aerobics would be more convenient for me, since I could do them under the trees which were right by my house. So the museum representative taught me how to do aerobics. It was good fun until some of the women on the excavation team saw me doing it and teased me. Apparently, it was a woman's sport. I didn't know if this was true or not, but I decided to tell my friend that I would give up aerobics. Then one afternoon, she called me again. I couldn't say anything and joined her. During the exercise, I asked her why we were doing it. She told me that it was to keep fit and to lose weight. I told her that I was quite fit and skinny. Indeed, I needed to put some weight on. If I carried on, my bones would start crumbling. So I told her that it would be better if I first gained some weight and then did some aerobics.

Anyway, as I left the temsilci, I watched the excavation team going up and down the mound. However, Ian wasn't around. I asked one of the team called David[2] and found out that Ian was ill. I wanted to visit him, but I didn't know how to speak. Even though David was English he spoke very good Turkish. So he taught me how to say "get well soon." He even wrote it down on a piece of paper to remind me. I knew that I wouldn't forget it, but I took the paper with me just in case. I was expecting Ian to be in bed, but when I went to his room, he was working on his computer. I was amazed that he was working even when ill. I felt sorry for him as I knew that at that time his wife and twins weren't there. It must be hard to get ill away from your own home. Nevertheless, he was still working instead of having a rest. I wondered if his work was more important than his health. While I was thinking about these things, Ian noticed me. Then I realized that I had forgotten the words David had told me. Ian was waiting for me to speak but I couldn't say anything for a few minutes. Suddenly I remembered the paper which David gave me. I passed it to Ian and he thanked me. He seemed to have enjoyed my visit.

After a while, Ian got better. One day, he was coming down to the dig house from the mound. He seemed quite strange and I couldn't understand whether he was upset or not. Actually, I had never seen him upset before. He often looks very calm. I thought that something was wrong. After dinner, Ian asked the excavation team to gather. He also asked the guards to join them. I was quite nervous, since he never called us for the regular meetings that he had with the excavation team. What was going on? He told us that somebody had made a clay figurine and pretended to find it on site. He didn't want this kind of joke to be made ever again, because it could cause all sorts of problems. Ian was right. If we are to work at such an important place as Çatalhöyük, we have to work seriously. The only thing that I couldn't understand however, was why Ian included the guards in the meeting. I can't even draw a figurine, never mind make one. Once again, I thought of a story to explain this. A government representative gathers nine village headmen[3] to have a meeting, but ten of them turn up. He is confused and asks why there are nine villages but ten headmen. One of the headmen says that his son is also the headman in his village. So I realized that I had become a headman.

16 Things start to go wrong

When I started my shift again after a week off, I saw some people working around my house, investigating the soil. One of them was called Mehmet İnce and like me he did extra work such as buying and selling cars. He wanted to buy my car and pay at a fixed date and I accepted his offer. He said that he would pay for the car within the next five months. When the season at Çatalhöyük was over, I went to see Mehmet to get my payment. He said that he didn't have any money and asked for more time. There was nothing I could do, so I gave him a little more time. When the deadline was over, I went to visit him again but he wasn't there. He had run away! I tried to find him, but it wasn't possible. So I decided to try to get my car back by seeking legal help. After a while, I found that my car was in a town about 150 km away from my village. I went there and managed to get my car back, but I am sure that a new car would have cost me less, what with all the traveling and the legal fees. However, the money wasn't that important. I wanted the car back to put a stop to his dishonest behavior.

Dealing with this problem affected me both emotionally and financially. I had to be more careful from now on. So I decided to take a break from doing trade. Anyway, the days at Çatalhöyük were becoming more exciting. Ian had invited a lot of journalists, TV reporters, and others to a press day at the site.[1] Everybody was working very hard. When the big day arrived, Ian presented the objects that had been found and took the visitors around the site. There were a lot of people. It felt like Çatalhöyük was alive again. As we got back from the mound, Ian told us that he wanted to have another meeting with the team. I couldn't understand why he wanted to have a meeting now. When the government representative told me not to let anybody into the site, I realized that something was definitely wrong. Ian looked very upset. I don't think that I have ever seen him like that before. At the meeting, we found out that a small object[2] had gone missing. Even though he knew that nobody on the team or working at the site was responsible for this incident, we had to wait for the gendarme to come and investigate. The whole team was very upset. Was this the result of all our efforts? We had been getting ready for this particular day for ages and we were all tired. The best thing to relieve our tiredness would have been to see some happy visitors. But instead, we had all become more upset and tired. Now I want to give my opinion about this incident. If I knew who had taken the object, I would explain to that person how stupidly he had acted. I want to say no more. After the gendarmes had gone, we all got back to work. I was impressed that everybody had helped the gendarme. I guess they all knew that there would be some investigation after such an incident. There is a saying in Turkish: "One insane person throws a stone into a well; a thousand sane people can't manage to get it out."

After the financial struggles I had experienced due to the cafe and my car, I thought that the best option would be to work in my field when I didn't guard Çatalhöyük. So I opened a watering well in the field. It was going to be good to work there, because I didn't have any money left to invest. I was quite upset, but there was nothing to do. I tried to keep my hopes positive and thought that the money I would earn from the crops would help me. So, I planted some beets.[3] I was working in the field every other week. The rest of my time I was guarding Çatalhöyük. One day, a friend called Cemil who worked at the police station came to visit the site. While we were chatting, I found out that he wanted to sell his car. I told him what had happened to me and asked if he would sell his car for the money which I would get from selling the beets. He said that since it was me, he would sell his car and receive the payment on a fixed date. I bargained the price down to 9300 DM[4]. After a month, another friend called Ahmet Sılay wanted to buy my car.

This is how I met Ahmet. One afternoon, the project minibus had an accident on its way to Çumra. I was at home. The driver came to find me, looking very panicky. He told me that he had had an accident. We were all very upset. When he calmed down, we went to see the accident. There was a taxi underneath the minibus. We couldn't understand where the taxi came from. The luckiest thing was that there was nobody inside the taxi. Later on, I found out that the taxi belonged to Ahmet Sılay. He had lost control of his car when a tire burst and had ended up in the canal. That was how the two cars ended up in the same place. I still can't understand how those accidents happened, though. First, a taxi had an accident. Then, our minibus had an accident in exactly the same place. Was this a coincidence? I don't think so! How come two different vehicles have different accidents at the same place, within 20 minutes? Okay, let's say this is a coincidence. But as a result of these accidents, I met Ahmet and sold my car to him, since his car was completely smashed. I wish that these cars hadn't had accidents and I had never met Ahmet. You will find out about the problems this friendship caused me later in the book.

Anyway, I asked him how he planned to pay for the car. He said that he would pay for the car when he sold his beets. After bargaining with him, I sold the car for 10,500 DM. So, I had made a profit of 1200 DM. It was nice to start trading again, but I had to look after my beets well and sell them for a good price at the end of the season. I was working hard not to re-experience the difficult days I had had in the past. I was much younger then and had the energy to fight problems that came up. Now I was not as energetic as I had been. Nevertheless I would never give up, since the future of my wife and the children depended on me. The thing that I was worried about was that while I was earning good money I didn't save it up. If I had saved some money, I wouldn't have been in this situation. Now I can only dream about those prosperous days. However, I am not upset as I keep remembering the fun days. I want to share one of those fun days with you.

One day, my friend Mevlüt called, asking if I wanted to go for a picnic. I agreed since I didn't have anything else to do. It was such a good idea. When we went to the picnic place, I realized that I didn't quite fit. They all had girlfriends and I was on my own. They started having fun as they got drunk while I kept sitting silent. Then a female friend called Ayşe asked me why I wasn't happy. I decided to tell her a little story to explain my feelings.

> Once upon a time, a villager went to visit the sheikh. When he arrived at the sheikh's house, he saw that everyone was sitting around the faraş ocağı (or oven) chatting.[5] The sheikh noticed the villager and invited him nearer the oven. As they were having a very nice conversation, nobody noticed that the villager's dress had caught fire in the oven and had started to burn. The villager tried to get the attention of the sheikh, but the sheikh thought that the dress was on fire as a result of the bright conversation they were having. So he ignored the villager. Finally, the villager shouted out and jumped into the garden pool to extinguish the fire.

"So, Ayşe," I said, "I am also on fire, but there isn't a swimming pool around here."

Ayşe told me that she was going to find a pool for me so we got into the car. We went to the city to pick up a female friend of hers. I had sex with her friend for the rest of the day. After this, Ayşe and I became very close friends and always called each other "my sheikh." I also got along well with her friend and our relationship carried on for quite a while. When I met Ayşe again, she asked me if I was still seeing her friend. Even though I was, I said no as I didn't want to upset her. She said that it was good that I didn't see her friend anymore, because she had AIDS. I was very worried when I heard this. I had been seeing her for about a year and we were having a good time. I quickly left Ayşe. I didn't know what to do, so I decided to visit my close friend Ahmet Parmak. I told him the situation. He tried to calm me down, but I was in such a pain. He suggested that we go to the hospital to get my blood tested. I told the nurse that I wanted to get a blood test. She asked me what for. I couldn't say AIDS, but Ahmet was brave enough to say it. The nurse pretended that everything was okay and started taking my blood sample. Then the doctor arrived. He asked me whether I felt exhausted. I said yes. He told me not to worry as everything would be clear after the blood test. It was going to take four hours. So we decided to leave. I was very upset. I asked Ahmet if he could stay with me, since I didn't want to be on my own that day. He said okay and we went drinking. Since I was quite upset, I got drunk very quickly. After a while, Ahmet told me it was time to go. When we arrived at the hospital, the test was ready. I looked at the paper, but couldn't understand anything. I asked the nurse and she said that everything was fine. I didn't believe her and started arguing that they must have mixed up the blood samples. The doctor came and told me that no one else had come for an AIDS test that day. So the samples could not have got mixed up. I was just fine. I kept arguing that he couldn't know better than my sheikh. He got confused. Of course, how the hell could sheikhs know about the AIDS disease? He didn't know that my sheikh was different, though. He got quite angry and asked me who my sheikh was. I told him that it wasn't his business and that he had to find some medicine for my illness. I think that he realized that I was drunk. So he asked Ahmet to take me home. Since I was drunk, I couldn't feel happy about being healthy. But later on, I felt over the moon. One day, my female friend wanted to see me.

However, I couldn't have sex and told her that I had the AIDS disease. She also ran to the hospital to get tested and she found she was fine. When I met Ayşe, I told her that we didn't have the AIDS disease. She said that she knew it. She hadn't wanted me to spend more time with her friend, so she had made up a little joke. I couldn't be angry with her. Nowadays, I don't have time for these kinds of games. I only focus on working hard.

One day, the water got cut off at the excavation house. I called the fire brigade to ask them if they could send some water to the site. They agreed and told me to call them again if we needed more water. While I was waiting for the water, two young boys came to the site. As I started talking to them, the fire brigade arrived. I asked the boys to wait for me for a while. They said that they would walk around the site. I told them that it was forbidden for people to visit the site on their own. They said that they would go back to work and visit the site later. I thanked them and went to help fill the dig house tank with water. After the fire brigade left, I came back to my house. Even though the boys had said they were going to leave, their bikes were still there. First of all, I wondered whether they had left their bikes and walked. Then, something told me to go up to the mound. When I went up to the site, I saw them sitting by the excavation area. I was slightly pissed off, since I had told them not to walk around on their own. I walked toward them and asked why they didn't wait for me. Now that I was there, I could guide them around. One of them said that they had walked around the whole site and now had to go back to work. I said okay, but while we were going back, one of the boys said that he wanted to visit the other excavation areas. I asked if they had not been there yet. They said that they had been, but they wanted to see it again. Despite getting angry, I decided to take them to the excavation area on the smaller northern hill.[6] I wasn't saying anything. Usually, I would try to give some information for the visitors,[7] but this time I didn't want to.

We stayed there for a while. Then one of them said that he didn't like it there, and they wanted to go back to where they had just come from. I started to get really angry with them. I told them that I didn't have time for them, since I had a lot of work to do. As we were going down, one of them asked if I knew whose son he was. I told him that I really didn't care whose son he was. Everybody was equal for me. They got on their bikes and went a short distance. I could hear them swearing at me in the distance. When I saw that they weren't going to leave easily, I got into my car and drove toward them. At this, they started running away. In spite of my having achieving what I wanted, I thought that it would be hard if every rich man had sons like these.

17 The situation worsens

Luckily, I did grow the beets on time and took them to the factory. When spring came I heard that the factory had started paying the farmers. Since there were a lot of beet farmers, the bank put all the villages in order and when our turn came we went and collected our money. I also had to collect the money for the car which I had sold to Ahmet Sılay. When I visited him, he told me that he hadn't got his money yet, but that his village was going to get paid in three days' time. So he was going to pay me in three days. I agreed and went to the police station to pay my debt to Cemil. When I returned to my village, I felt very happy. It was nice to see the result of my efforts. My main aim was to work harder to increase the standards of my life. Anyway, Ahmet called me after three days saying that the bank was very crowded and he still hadn't receive his money. But if I wanted to, he could transfer his money from his account to mine. I agreed and went to the bank to get my money. While I was waiting in the queue, Ahmet called me inside. I left the queue and sat down with a friend of his who worked at the bank. Ahmet worked for the same bank, but at another branch in town. I asked him what he was doing here. He told me that he needed some papers as the two branches worked together. He was in a rush, but he was also going to sort my transfer out before he left. While he was dealing with my paperwork, I chatted to his friend. After a while, Ahmet asked me to sign some papers. Since the money was to be paid into my name, I signed the papers. When the cashier called my name, I went and collected the money. However, it wasn't 10,500 DM. I told Ahmet that the money was short. He told me that he was going to pay the rest in a few days. I said okay and went back to the village.

Dear readers, this situation ended up causing me a lot of trouble. I will tell you everything very clearly. I hope nobody else experiences what I have been through. I am one of those people who go through terrible pain in this world. I guess that it is my fate even though I have never been bad to anyone. But I won't be alone anymore. I will forget about this terrible pain as I will share it with my readers. I hope that after my book is published, some people will regret they caused me so much pain. Let me tell you the rest of the story.

I came back to the village and carried on my work at Çatalhöyük as well as in my field. One day, two men came to the site telling me that they wanted to talk to me. We went to the cafe and I answered their questions. They asked me why I took money from Ahmet. I told them that he bought my car. As I found out later, these men were inspectors working for the bank. After our chat, they told me that they suspected Ahmet had committed a crime. I asked them what that had to do with me. They said it had nothing to do with me, but they had to check. I never thought badly of Ahmet. I always believed in him. One day I was waiting to finish my shift at Çatalhöyük. I could feel that something was wrong. When I went home, I talked to my wife about it. She told me that I was working hard, so maybe going away would make me feel better. She could be right. So I decided to go to the seaside. I packed my bag and got on the road. After a while, I stopped to have a cup of tea. However, instead of feeling better, I started feeling worse. I couldn't understand what was happening to me. I arrived at the seaside at midnight. I booked a room at a hotel and thought that if I drank a little, I would feel better. Even though I was hungry, I kept drinking. The only thing that I wanted was to get drunk and fall asleep. But it was impossible. The more I drank, the worse I felt. It was 4 in the morning and I thought that I was going to die. I left the hotel to go to the seashore. It was very quiet. I took my shoes off and walked barefoot in the sea. I found

relief in the waves. It seemed like I forgot about my problems as I watched the sea for a while. Then I remembered
a scene from a movie. There was a mermaid in this movie.
I wondered if that mermaid was real. And if she was, I
wished that she would come and take me to the sea. I tried
to listen for any sound coming from the sea just in case it
belonged to the mermaid. But the only thing that I could
hear was the sound of the waves. Maybe there were no
mermaids except in movies. I didn't care, however. I was
going to wait for her until she turned up. I was used to
waiting for things anyway as it was my job. But I wasn't
the only one waiting for things. Some wait for their lov-
ers, some for their youth, some to die, and some to be born.
I was waiting for my mermaid. Maybe she was waiting to
be born. If she was born and saw me, she could share my
pain and take me to the sea with her. I am sure you all
think that she wouldn't come, but I was determined to wait
for her. She was going to come and rescue me. Maybe she
was already calling me, but I couldn't hear. The sound of
the waves was stopping me from hearing her. The waves
were right, though. Who wouldn't be jealous of my mermaid? Maybe they were in love with her and therefore
didn't want to share her with me. As I thought this, I stood
up and shouted toward the waves, saying, "Hey, you
waves! I leave my mermaid to you. Look after her! I
couldn't understand what you were trying to say and I
know that you also didn't understand me. The only thing
I know is that I am in terrible pain and I don't know why."

I left the seashore with these thoughts and got into my
car. I must have fallen asleep. I woke up around 9 a.m.,
feeling very hot. After having my breakfast, I decided to
go back to the village as I couldn't wait any longer. My
wife was surprised when she saw me. She asked me why
I had come back early. I said that I was bored and couldn't
work out what was wrong with me. I was worried that
something very bad was going to happen to me. I left the
house to go to my cafe.

When I arrived back at the cafe, Mustafa told me that the police had come asking for me. I immediately called the police station. They asked me to go there as soon as possible. I thought that this was it. This was the reason I had been feeling restless. I must have sensed it. When I arrived at the police station, they put me in jail. I didn't know what I was guilty of. When I asked the policemen, they told me that I would find out tomorrow. Smoking wasn't allowed in the jail. I thought that I was going to lose my mind. The head officer arrived around midnight. I told him that I wasn't guilty of anything, and I hadn't done anything bad. I said that if I stayed here any longer, I would lose my mind. The officer let me stand outside the jail for a bit. As I lit a cigarette, I wondered why I was there. I didn't think that I had done anything wrong. There must have been a misunderstanding. At that moment, the policemen brought in Ahmet Sılay. I was shocked. When I asked why he was there, I realized that this situation was related to the car I had sold him. They had arrested me for that. Ahmet didn't seem to want to talk to me about it. In the morning, Ahmet and I were seen by an attorney. First, he talked to Ahmet. Then he called me in. He asked me why I had withdrawn illegal money from the bank. I neither accepted this accusation nor defended myself, because I knew that I wasn't guilty. I only told the truth. "I didn't take dirty money from Ahmet. I had bought a car from my friend Cemil and later I sold it to Ahmet to be paid at a fixed date. When the deadline arrived, Ahmet told me that he had transferred the money into my account. I agreed and went to the bank to withdraw the money. Ahmet was also at the bank and told me that he was going to arrange the papers for me. Then he brought me the papers to be signed. I sold the car for 10,500 DM, but the money I got was less than this amount. After one month, Ahmet paid the rest of the money." Despite my telling the truth, the attorney sent us to the judge. I told the judge exactly the same things. The judge decided that I didn't have to be under arrest while my case was being looked at. In the meantime, Ahmet had admitted that he was the one who was guilty but the judge decided there should be a second trial for me. So Ahmet went to jail and I came back home. My family was very happy, but I still wasn't free. I could only be free after the second case. As I waited for the trial, I felt terrible every day. I was so embarrassed that I had been accused of fraud. I realised how happy I had been before this had happened.

When the day arrived, I went to the trial. The judge asked his questions in a very understanding way. Apparently, the money which I withdrew from the bank didn't belong to Ahmet, but to someone called Sadrettin Gökkaya. When Ahmet made the transfer, he used Sadrettin's name instead of mine. Because I had signed the papers without reading them, I appeared guilty. I really hadn't known, though. If I had read the papers, I wouldn't have signed them. I know that I should have read the papers, but how many people would read the papers before they signed? I really didn't intend anything bad. Anyway, the judge asked Sadrettin if he had a complaint against Ahmet. He said yes. Then he asked him if he had a complaint against me. Sadrettin said no. The judge decided to send the case to a higher court. When we came out, I asked Ahmet's solicitor if I had a chance to get out of this mess. He said that I wasn't really guilty.

Anybody might make the same mistake. Even Ahmet had said that I wasn't guilty. So maybe I would be free in the end. I came home, feeling very happy. It was good that the next trial would take place in the city, since my lawyer friend Sermet Öten lived there. I thought that he would defend me and get me out of this mess. As I waited for the next trial, Ahmet's father sold his tractor as well as his field to pay the money back to the bank. I felt so much better, because it meant that Ahmet didn't have any debt anymore. Months later, I found out that the bank manager was also aware of what was going on. So he had called

Ahmet's father, saying that he had to pay the money back, otherwise Ahmet could go to jail. While everybody was trying to cover for Ahmet, Sadrettin Gökkaya wrote a letter to the Ankara branch of the bank, asking for his account to be checked. If Sadrettin had waited one more week, Ahmet's father and the bank manager would have covered up the whole thing.

Finally it was my last trial and I went to the city. I was quite relaxed since Sermet was with me and I really trusted him. During the trial, the judge asked me why I withdrew 6 billion TL from the bank. I was quite confused not knowing where this amount came from. I told the judge that I didn't withdraw that amount. Then he started shouting at me, saying that I was lying. I told him that I only took 10,500 DM from the bank. He asked Ahmet if I took 6 billion TL from him and Ahmet said no. After paying me, he had taken the rest of the money. The judge postponed the case to another day. The next day, I went to Çatalhöyük to start my shift. However, I was very stressed. I didn't understand why I was feeling like that so I called Sermet to talk about how I felt. He said that it was okay if I didn't want to attend the next trial since he had the power of attorney for me and could defend me even if I wasn't there. I told him that I would be there in any circumstances. Feeling worse, I started waiting for the case to come up again. Every now and then I thought that this wasn't the worst time I had have in my life.

One day Mevlit, a friend from the army, and Metin whom I met when I was a taxi driver, came to visit me. My nephew Mustafa and I were sitting in the garden. They said that they were going to fish and asked if we wanted to join them. Anyway, we went to the lakeside and found a quiet place for fishing. We set up our barbecue, so that we could eat the fish as we caught it. We all seemed very happy. There were two fishing boats by us in the lake and we wanted to take one of them for a short tour. Mevlit, Mustafa, and I got in the boat. Metin didn't want to join us, since he didn't know how to swim. We were trying to get the boat to move and we didn't care that it was filling with water as we thought that we knew how to swim. The water level increased and we decided to swim back to the shore. Mevlit was in front with Mustafa, and I was following. Suddenly, I noticed that Mustafa wasn't a very confident swimmer. The lake was denser than the sea and it was quite tiring to swim in it. When Mustafa told me that he was very tired, I shouted to Metin to get the other boat to help Mustafa. I tried to encourage Mustafa to swim while Metin was coming to rescue us. Mustafa told me that he wasn't able to swim anymore and he held onto me. Then both of us went under the water. I pulled him up and told him to let go of me but keep moving in the water. He tried to swim a little more, but then gave up and sank again. I wasn't going to leave him alone even if we died in the end. So I dove into the water and caught Mustafa by his feet. When I heard him splashing the water, I knew that he was able to breathe again. When I got Mustafa above the water, I started feeling very tired. I imagined my children, since I thought that I was going to die. Suddenly, Mustafa slipped away from me and I realized that Metin must have arrived and taken him. They helped me to get on the boat. I asked Metin why he had taken so long. He looked embarrassed, saying that he didn't know how to drive the boat, and so Mevlit had helped him. I was so happy to be alive!

I felt better when I thought about these memories and went to the city again to attend the second trial. Ahmet's father was also there. I asked him why he had paid the money back. Apparently, Ahmet told him that I wasn't guilty, so he had to pay it back to clean up his son's mess. He told me not to worry. "You will not be charged," he said. "We all know that you aren't guilty. It is a shame that you had to be involved in this mess." I said that it wasn't a problem. But I couldn't understand why Ahmet did such a thing. Anyway, we attended the case. Cemil said that he sold me his car, and after a month I sold it to Ahmet. Ahmet's cousin Ibrahim and a friend of his, who were my witnesses when I sold the car, were also questioned by the judge. Unlike the first trial, nobody accused me but I had to wait there while Ahmet's case was heard.

In fact, Ahmet had more than one case against him, and the judge postponed my trial until the other cases became clear. I attended every trial, without saying anything. As I was waiting for the last case, I carried on working at Çatalhöyük. One day, I was guiding some tourists around the site when a tour bus arrived. I asked them either to join us or to wait until I had finished the first tour. They said that they would wait for me. When we came down the mound, I saw these tourists getting undressed by the fountain near my house. Some women didn't even have a bra on. I quickly approached them and asked what they were doing. They said that they wanted to have a shower. I didn't want to say no, but I didn't want them to be naked in the open either. I told them that it would be better if they took a shower in the toilet. They agreed and started lining up. However, they were still naked. So I decided to cut the hose into four pieces and connected them to the fountain, to the toilet, to the kitchen, and to the sink. This way, I minimized the time everybody took to have a shower and prevented any local people noticing.

When the big day arrived, I went to Konya to attend the last trial. There were a lot of people waiting around. They all looked very sad. I knew that it wasn't easy. Everybody makes mistakes, but I wished that their lives didn't get into a mess as a result. While I was thinking about these things, I heard my name being called. The judge started talking about the laws but I couldn't understand anything. Then I looked at Sermet and realized that I was in trouble. Sermet looked very upset. After the case was over, I waited for him to finish his other cases. When we finally arrived at his office, he told me that the judge had found me guilty. I was destroyed. He said that the judge had given us another month to prepare my last defense. I asked him if that was it. Even though he told me that there was still hope, I didn't stop worrying. I thought that I should tell everything to my director at the museum. I was in deep thought while I went to the Konya Mevlana Museum.[1] I was trying to work out how to start telling him that I had been found guilty of fraud. What would my director, friends, and colleagues think? But I had to tell them despite feeling very embarrassed. The director was in his office. Once he summoned me into his room, I told him that I had important things to tell him. He listened to everything I said. He told me not to be ashamed of anything, since it could have happened to anyone. He certainly believed in me and sent me back to work.

I was finding it very hard to carry on my life in the village as I was feeling very ashamed in front of my family and friends. For the first time, it seemed like the days were going by very slowly. Nevertheless, I was very happy when I was at Çatalhöyük. One day, İsmail Polat who had built the excavation house, came to visit me with his nephew. He was a great man and that is why I respected him very much. He used to work with a young boy called Galip. Apparently, Galip was quite weak and couldn't handle some of the work he was given. İsmail told him not to stop coming to work, since he had decided that Galip wasn't strong enough for the job. Galip was angry and complained that İsmail didn't want him to come because they were going to slaughter a sheep and have some meat for lunch. İsmail told him to come and have some meat, but that was it. He was too young to handle such a job, so he was going to fire him. Galip came to have some food the next day and asked me to talk to İsmail and persuade him not to fire him. He needed to earn money. I encouraged him to talk to İsmail himself but said that I would support him if needed. After a while, İsmail called me, asking about Galip. I told him how genuine and honest he was. As a result Galip got his job back even though İsmail did the difficult jobs that Galip was supposed to do.

Anyway, being such a nice person, İsmail asked me why I looked so sad. I told him what had happened. When his nephew Şenasi heard my story, he said that I should not be trusted. Suddenly my world fell apart, since Şenasi was one of my best friends. I felt scared, thinking that everybody else would think the same. I left them as I went up the mound, imagining the Neolithic people. An archaeologist friend told me that I had similarities with a Neolithic person. He was possibly right. Once, Ian had found a skeleton in an area of rubbish.[2] The person had been disabled in life. Ian told us that this person may have been excluded from the community because of his disability. I wondered if my fate was to be like this person. I started imagining him and his life nine thousand years ago and how he became disabled. In my opinion, he went outside Çatalhöyük to hunt. He got hurt while he was fighting with a bull. If he had defeated the bull, he could have proved his power. Unfortunately, things didn't go how he expected and when he returned to Çatalhöyük, the community didn't accept him. They were probably upset about him being defeated. I don't know if they sent him to the rubbish area or if he left of his own will. It is hard for a disabled person to find food on his own. So if nobody gave him food, he must have gone to the rubbish area to find some. When I put myself in his place, I wanted to say, "I got hurt because of my pride. And when I returned to my city to be looked after, my people ignored me. What should I do? I beg help from everyone, but no one wants to help me. How can I manage to live like this? If I go to the rubbish area, maybe I can find something to eat." Then he went there to wait until he died. At this point, I have a question for Ian Hodder. "You told us that the Neolithic people lived in equality. Were there other people who were excluded from the community apart from the disabled?"[3] It is interesting that even though nobody understood this person at the time, nine thousand years later we can feel how he felt. How come?

I would have loved to live in those times to be able to understand the Neolithic people better. Nevertheless, we are both lucky, since his memory is kept alive by Ian while mine will be by my book.

I missed the last trial since it was my shift at Çatalhöyük. So I waited for a phone call from Sermet to find out the result. It was raining heavily and I was hoping for the best. The farmers love rain, because it means prosperity. I wondered if the rain would bring me good news. I had to wait. Soon, Sermet called. The judge had not believed my defense and therefore had given me a jail sentence of 25 months as well as a 14 million TL fine. That was it for me! Sermet told me not to worry too much, since he was going to try to appeal. It was clear that the sky was crying for me. I went out for a walk, wondering how I was going to explain this to my family and friends. When I got back to my house, Sermet called again. I felt slightly relieved as he said that the appeal might bring good results. It seemed like the only thing that I could do was wait.

My life wasn't the same. My friends were saying that I hardly smiled, nevermind laughed. Even the excavation team could tell something was wrong. Being a fun person once, they used to draw cartoons of me looking happy and smiling. That summer, I looked very sad in all the cartoons. Knowing that I worried my friends, I tried to hide my sadness. I am not sure how successful I was, but I thought that I didn't have the right to upset other people. I decided to keep working and not get involved in anything that might be illegal. One of my memories which I want to tell you now is a good example of what I am trying to say.

One day, my nephew Mustafa came to ask for a favor. His job was to sell car radiators and he asked me if we could use my car to deliver the radiators to Edirne. I agreed and we started our journey. When we arrived at Babaeski, which is a small town near Edirne, we delivered some of the radiators to the shops and decided to leave the others for the next day. Since we had the whole evening, we went to visit one of Mustafa's shop neighbors called Hasan. After working in Konya for years, Hasan's business had failed and therefore he had moved to Babaeski to start a new business. It was nice to hear that he was doing well. Hasan didn't leave us that evening. As some of his friends also joined us, the atmosphere became really nice. It seemed as if Hasan fitted very well into the community. When we said that we wanted to go to bed, he offered his own, but we said that we would sleep in my car. Around 1 a.m., someone knocked on the car window. It was some of Hasan's friends, asking to borrow my car to pick up a whore from the nearby town. I refused saying that we were sleeping in the car. They said that my nephew could sleep in Hasan's shop while I went with them to get the whore. They were planning to bring her by force, if she didn't want to come. I said no and got back in the car. During all this, Mustafa woke up and we decided to leave. I had many female friends, but I never asked them to do anything by force. A sensible person wouldn't try to have a friendship or a relationship by force. Anyway, we carried on driving to find a safe place to sleep. On the way, we saw a factory with a crowd outside even though it was very late at night. We stopped there to have some tea. While we were waiting for the teas to come, a man sat down at our table and showed us an erotic picture of a woman in a newspaper which was already on the table. He said that she was the waiter's mother. So, wouldn't we want to have her, instead of the tea? Despite hearing what he said, the waiter ignored him. I was very embarrassed, though. I didn't talk for a while. Then the man called the waiter saying that we wanted to have his mother, so we needed to talk about the money. Just as I was getting ready for a fight, he pulled out his knife. I guess he realized my intention and he was trying to scare me off. I told Mustafa that we should go back to the car. Once we got to the car, I picked up a heavy tool. I was also getting ready for a fight. Mustafa told me not to do anything stupid, since we were the strangers here and nobody would support us. However, I didn't want to listen. The waiter looked so upset and I had to defend him. I told Mustafa to leave, but he said that he wouldn't leave me on my own. While we were going back to the cafe, the waiter stopped us saying that the man was a psycho. If we picked a fight with him, we wouldn't be doing him any favor, but would create more trouble for him after we left. He was right. So we decided to leave immediately.

When I got back to the village, I found that my son had become ill and that my brother had helped my family as much as he could in my absence. Since I was very worried about him, I went to see him first. Luckily he was feeling much better. However the pain I felt due to his illness made me think about the baby skeleton that had been found at Çatalhöyük.[4] The baby was thought to have died around the age of 5 months. When they found her, she was wearing a necklace and a bracelet made of bone. In my opinion, she was very precious to her parents. In my village, newly married couples get pregnant shortly after getting married and all the family start getting ready for the baby's birth. For instance, they knit shoes, hats, clothes, blankets, and so on, and in spite of working in the field all day, they don't complain a bit. I wondered if the parents of this baby had made this bracelet and necklace for her while waiting for her birth. And when she died, they had to bury her. I really feel for them. They must have felt destroyed. Now I want to ask Ian Hodder! We all became very emotional when you found this baby skeleton. I am wondering if it is possible to use DNA testing to find out whether her parents had another baby. We really would like to know. Even if they could have had another baby, we are ready to feel the sadness.[5]

I want to focus on the skeletons a little bit more. When a Neolithic person died, he/she was buried under the floor of his/her house. We also know that they were short and skinny people. Ian has told us all about the Neolithic people. I know that his team uses the most developed excavation techniques at Çatalhöyük. Therefore we would like to find out more things about the site. For instance, Ian told us that there were five or six people living in one house. I wonder if there was a family structure. Were the members of the family respectful to one another? How would a person make a choice for a wife or a husband? Let's say a man found a girlfriend. Who was she? If she was the neighbor's daughter, would he bring her into his house or would he move into her house? I am very curious about such matters. If every male or female brings a partner into the house, wouldn't the number of people living in the same house increase? By studying the bones, they can even find out about what they ate. Moreover, I wonder if there was any blood relation between the people who lived together. How were they having sex? Considering that there wasn't any birth control in those times, they must have had a baby every year. If a family lived in a house for 50 years, this would mean 50 children. Ian told us that most babies died right after their birth, whereas some died within the first ten years of their lives. And if a baby managed to live for ten years, his or her life could be as long as 70–80 years. I would like to ask Ian whether there were incest relationships within the family or not? Would a baby have more than one father? Would the couples have sex when they desired or just during the certain periods as a form of birth control? All in all, it would be interesting to find out more about how the Neolithic people reproduced.[6] Funnily enough, I asked my mother about this. She said that she didn't know much about the people of Çatalhöyük, but she had heard that they were our ancestors. "I don't think they had incestuous relationships," she said. "So, don't go around asking such questions. You might be offending their spirits!"

One day, Ahmet Sılay's brother called, while I was at Çatalhöyük. He told me that the result of the appeal was that both Ahmet and I had been found guilty. I was shocked and I knew that the gendarmes would be here to arrest me at any minute. I never want to remember that day again. I asked my nephew Mustafa to go and let the people know in the village. I needed to find someone else to guard Çatalhöyük while I was in jail. So I told my nephew everything I knew about the site and how hard he should work. After my shift, I went back to the village. It was very hard to explain the situation to my family, but they understood. I didn't understand why the judge had found me guilty, since I had only told him the truth. I really didn't deserve this punishment. Believe me, my readers, I still feel terrible while I write these sentences. I had not done anything wrong on purpose. Anyway, first I decided to spend a nice evening with my family. My plan was to go to the museum in the morning, tell everything to my director, and put forward my nephew Mustafa Ferahkaya as the new guard at Çatalhöyük. Then I was going to make copies of my defense paper and throw them around the courthouse before committing suicide from the top floor. I felt like I didn't want to live anymore. I was a fraud and therefore couldn't look anyone in the face. So death seemed the best option for me. Knowing this, I tried to spend a very nice evening with my children.

I couldn't sleep at all that night. I knew that tomorrow I was going to fall into an eternal sleep. The next morning, I couldn't eat anything. Just as I was about to leave, my sister-in-law called, saying that there was a letter for me, possibly from the bank. It was a credit card bill. Nobody wants to die with debts. So, I went back home to get some money to pay off my bill. It seemed that my wife had sensed what I was planning to do, since she begged me to have a cup of tea. I didn't want to hurt her and said okay. Then I heard the gendarmes arriving. I didn't want to go with them, because I had a lot of things to do beforehand. I wished that I hadn't listened to my wife. As I was waiting inside, the head gendarme asked me to come out. I told him that I had to do a few things before letting

myself be arrested. He said that if I went with them
straightaway, I could ask the head policeman for permission. There was no way that I could argue with them. So
I went downstairs and put my wrists forward for him to
put handcuffs on, but he said that there was no need for
it. When we arrived at the police station, the head of police didn't let me go. The only option was to call the museum, tell them the situation, and suggest that my nephew
be the new guard at Çatalhöyük. After I had done that,
the gendarmes drove me to the prison. I can't tell you how
terrible I felt. Once we were at the prison, they took away
my ID card and driver's license. I was very scared even
though I didn't know why. As I went to my cell, I met
two men. One of them was called Kadir Kunt and the other
one was İsmail Sarıkula. They had been transferred from
the Konya prison.[7] İsmail asked me where I was from.
When I told him that I was from Küçükköy, he asked me
if I worked as a guard at Çatalhöyük. I was surprised. How
did he know that I was a guard? I said yes and asked him
if he knew me from before. He said no, but told me that
he had met Ahmet Sılay at the Konya prison. Apparently
Ahmet had mentioned to him that I had said I wasn't
guilty. I felt a little relieved, thinking that at least some
people thought that I was innocent. However I was very
sad, knowing that all these problems had affected my
ambition for Çatalhöyük. I started to feel like a blind person. Once upon a time, there was a blind man. One day,
he asked his friend to take him outside. His friend took
him to the edge of a mountain. The blind man asked his
friend to tell what he could see. He started saying that there
was a river around the mountain as well as a lot of trees
on it. There were no trees on another mountain behind.
Then the blind person interrupted, saying that his friend
did not know how to look at the beauty he saw. So he
started telling what he saw with his blind eyes. "The mountain with no trees could never have been very prosperous.
However, it wasn't its choice, especially given that there

was another mountain in front of it, full of healthy trees and always boasting."

Let's look at my own life. I really didn't know what I would be doing after I finished my prison sentence. I hoped that they would employ my nephew as a guard, so that when I left the prison, I could go and visit Çatalhöyük. I don't understand why, but my friend Mustafa disrupted my plan. He managed to get his brother employed instead of my nephew. He might have been right to want his brother as the guard, but then why did he not support my nephew when they needed a third guard? I guess if my nephew had started working there, I would still have been involved with Çatalhöyük in some way and this might have made Mustafa very uncomfortable.

One day, the prison guard called me saying that I had some visitors. When I went to the visitors' room, I saw my director, Erdoğan Erol, and some friends from the museum. You can't believe how happy I was. Obviously, I had gained their respect during my hard work at Çatalhöyük. However, I found it hard to look at my director in the face. He must have seen my embarrassment, since he didn't talk about what had happened at all. After he left, the guard told me that I had other visitors. I asked who they were and he asked me to guess. It would have been nice to see Ian. But it wasn't possible. He was a foreigner so how would he find his way all the way here? Then the guard asked if I had a guess yet. I said that it could be my boss, but it wasn't a very realistic guess. He smiled and said that nothing was impossible. It was my boss and some of his colleagues. I was shocked and wondered how I could present myself to them under these circumstances. I wished I could have died rather than seeing them here. They were all educated people. Even though I liked the idea of being respected by them, I didn't think that I deserved it. While I was thinking these things, my name was called. When I went to the visitor room, there they were—Ian, Shahina, Louise, Can, Ayfer, and Adnan.[8] I talked to all of them.

However, they all looked very sad which made me feel guiltier. I didn't have the right to upset them. They were all precious people and didn't have to worry about me.

In the end, I completed my sentence. Even though I didn't know why, I couldn't help crying when leaving the prison. I was very happy. My brother and nephew had come to pick me up. Just before we went to the car, I told my brother to wait a little. As I looked back at the prison, it seemed like the whole thing had never happened. It was like a horrible nightmare. I could hardly walk to the car. On the way home, my brother put my favorite song on the tape. I opened a beer as I had never felt this happy before. It felt like I was just born. I thought that all my problems had finally come to an end. But I was wrong! I will tell you why later on. Anyway, when we passed Çatalhöyük I told my brother to stop. He said that my family was waiting for me, so it would be better to go home first. I argued that I needed to see Çatalhöyük, since it was the source of my life. Once we got to the site, no one seemed to be there. I wanted to get out, but my brother stopped me saying that my Çatalhöyük wasn't there anymore. He said that I had to listen to him if I didn't want to get hurt. I said okay and we went home. All my family was there. Apart from me, everybody looked very happy. I was sad, because I had lost my job at Çatalhöyük. Even if they offered it to me again, I wouldn't go back, because this would make Mustafa's brother (who had taken my job as one of the guards) redundant. I wouldn't want to put anybody in trouble in order to achieve what I wanted. Even though this person was the brother of a friend who did not like me much, my intention was the same. I was planning to go back to being a farmer. I knew that it was going to be hard, since farming required some start-up money. So I decided to start working at my cafe. Every morning, I went to the cafe with my son. I hoped that the cafe would make more money than it had before. I made sure that nobody realized how desperate I was. The excavation team would often come to get some ice cream. Although I wasn't earning much from them, I was still feeling better. I carried on working at the cafe until the excavation team finished the season.

I want to tell you about the day I closed down the cafe for the winter. It was a very hot day and there was nobody around. My son, Mustafa Dural, and I were waiting at the cafe, in the hope that someone might turn up. When my son asked me why we were still there, even though we didn't earn any money, I tried to explain to him my intentions. I told him that Çatalhöyük was quite far away from the city. "If the tourists get thirsty, there is nowhere else but here to get some water. So it is always important to provide help for the tourists, even if we don't make any money."

I went to my friend Münir's office the same day, to get my computer fixed. There were also some other friends of his visiting. While we were having tea, Münir started joking with one of his friends, calling him "bold." I felt very sorry for the guy and I told him that I wished I was bold. He asked me why and I said that apparently a lot of women fancied bold men. When he said that he had never come across such women, I decided to tell him a story:

"One day, a villager brought his sick goat to the hodja,[9] asking him to pray for it. He said that his friends told him to give some medicine to the goat, but he trusted the hodja's prayer more. The hodja agreed to help, but added that he must also remember to give the medicine." So I told him to take precautions by creating a good "smell" for his boldness. He agreed and carried on by telling another story:

"This villager also had a cat. He had never let her out, just in case she got hurt. One of his neighbors told him that it wasn't good to keep the cat inside, and that if he smeared some gasoline on her and let her out, male cats wouldn't bother her. The villager did what the neighbor suggested and found that it worked. One day, the cat didn't come back home. He told his neighbor that his cat had got lost. The neighbor said that he saw her being dragged by two male cats as it seemed she had run out of gas." So the bold guy asked me what would happen if he ran out of nice smells, too. We all laughed!

18 Reaching the end

Dear readers, as I am approaching the end of my book, I realize how tired I am. This tiredness has nothing to do with writing this book, but with seeing my life not going the way I wanted. It feels like the summer is long gone and now I have to deal with the winter. To be honest, I don't believe that the summer will come back again. And even if it does, I don't think that I will be alive to see it. I only hope that none of you experiences a life like mine. Most of my friends have put me in difficult situations, just to get their own way. For instance, as I was trying to earn some money from farming, they cut off my water supply. By doing that, they not only hindered my work, but also affected my family. These people used to be my best friends, but I don't want to remember their names anymore. I only have a few real friends now and my main aim is to work as hard as possible until I die. I feel like a tired giraffe. When the lions attack a giraffe, they bite his feet to kill him, since they can't reach his body. The giraffe copes with the pain as long as he can, but then he gives up and dies. I will be the same. Then, I hope that the lions who made me suffer will remember me when they get attacked by the panthers.

From now on, I will be a 40-plus-year-old man with two tractors, a farm, and a cafe at Çatalhöyük. I don't want to think about my enemies anymore. I will tell you why. One day, a nanny takes the children to the zoo. When they visit the storks, the nanny says that the children were brought into the world by storks. The children giggle and think that they should tell their nanny the truth about babies. I don't think that there is any point. Nothing would change after a while. I know what would change my life, though. If I sell my cafe, my financial state would get better. However, Çatalhöyük is my only livelihood. To be honest, I wouldn't know what to do if I left it. I am in love with this place. I love my boss, I love my director, and I love my friends. If you remember, when my friend Kazım asked whether I would leave Çatalhöyük if a better job came up, I said NO WAY! Even if they fired me, I would still stay. Now I wonder why Kazım asked me that question. Did he sense that I was going to leave?

I see myself as a salmon fish sometimes. I started my life in a lake. Then I swam toward the endless seas. Here I am again, in the lake. Despite facing a lot of problems, I am trying to be strong and happy. I have a few dreams and I want to share them with you. I am not going to live in my house until I die. If I earn some money, I am going to build a small house by my cafe. It does not matter whether I guard the site or not. I can still keep an eye on it from the other side. And if you ever come to visit Çatalhöyük, I will be there waiting for you. If I am not around, don't worry! I probably have some work to do in my field and I will be back to Çatalhöyük soon. But if I don't come back, you should know that I am gone to my star which I owned on a lovely, starry night, and will never come back to this world.

THE END

Appendix: My tour of Çatalhöyük

Dear readers, as you know by now, I used to work as a guard at Çatalhöyük. I also used to guide the tourists around the site, because I believed that it was a part of my job. Even though it will only be imaginary, I invite you one last time to walk around Çatalhöyük with me. Welcome to you all!

First of all, we will go up onto the larger hill of the East Mound. Çatalhöyük is a Neolithic town which was lived in between 7400 and 6000 B.C. It was discovered by James Mellaart in 1958. The South Area you see in front of you was excavated by him between 1960 and 1965. Even though he said that there were 13 levels on the site, the current excavations revealed that there are more than 13 levels. After 1965, excavations stopped until 1993, when a team run by Professor Ian Hodder started new excavations. The cleaning work which you see here was achieved by Ian Hodder as well as by other archaeologists who came from different parts of the world. Unfortunately, this area wasn't under protection for a long time after 1965 and so it was eroded by the rain, wind, and snow. It is troubling that this area deteriorated, but there are also good things happening at Çatalhöyük and now you can see that a large part of the area is protected by a shelter that has stopped the erosion.

Now we will visit the small northern hill of the East Mound to have a look at the new excavations there. Once upon a time, the fields which you see on the plain to the east of the mound were full of trees and the Neolithic people used to hunt there. According to the excavations, they used to eat a lot of cattle and pig meat. In the upper layers fewer cattle and pig bones were found which meant that cattle and pig had become less available as time went by. As a tool to kill animals, they used something called "obsidian" (a volcanic stone) which they brought from Cappadocia and made into knives and arrow heads.

Çatalhöyük houses were made of mudbrick. Neolithic people made their own houses and lived in them for up to 70–100 years. Eventually, they would take all their belongings with them and fill the whole house with earth. They would build their houses on top of the walls of the destroyed houses and the houses would have no windows or doors. The hole which they would open on the roof would act as a chimney, window, and door. There were no streets or roads in the town and the people would use the roofs to move about.

The West Mound, which you can see over there, is small and the one we are visiting now is large. Apparently, the first settlement was founded here. But when more people came to settle at Çatalhöyük, the second mound started to be inhabited. Nearly eight thousand people lived at Çatalhöyük. The surveys around the mounds uncovered a large river and wetlands from which the Neolithic people got a lot of benefit. For example, they used reeds, hunted fish, and gathered bird eggs. But the people would also plant productive crops such as wheat.

Çatalhöyük is a very important Neolithic settlement. There are other Neolithic settlements all over the world such as in the Middle East and Europe. The ones in the Middle East go back 10,000 to 11,000 years, whereas Çatalhöyük is 9,000 years old. The earliest farming settlements in Europe are 8,000 years old. It is interesting that major wall paintings were only discovered at Çatalhöyük. If you ask why, the answer is still being looked for. Even the Guiness Book of World Records says that the first mural paintings were found at Çatalhöyük. But some people misunderstand this information. Actually, the first paintings were found in Palaeolithic caves, whereas the first paintings that were made on walls were found at Çatalhöyük. We can also say that important trade activities took place here. Things like timber and fruits would come from the Taurus Mountains, and sea shells would be supplied from the Mediterranean. This type of trade didn't involve the use of money, but the action of exchange. Neolithic people would use these shells to make necklaces and so on.

Now we will look at the current excavation work on the small northern hill. The work was started here by Ian Hodder's team in 1993. The area that you see is a house[1] and some skeletons were found under that platform. According to the studies that were undertaken on these skeletons, the Neolithic people were slim and of medium height (approx. 160 cm). The approximate life expectancy was about 35 years. However, many people lived up to the age of 60 or 70. The reason the life expectancy was low was that most deaths occurred during birth or within the first 10 years of life. Modern science also allows us to find out what the Neolithic people ate. For instance, they ate a variety of plants and meats, especially sheep and goat meat.

The skeletons are often found under the platforms of the houses, since when the Neolithic people died, they would get buried there. We may think that this is not a nice tradition. However, the Neolithic people believed that the soul of the dead would continue to live in the house together with the rest of the family. One time, they found a skeleton that was buried rather differently. The body was headless and the head was found at the base of a house post. Apparently, first they removed the head and then buried the body separately. This wasn't the general burial practice for all the bodies. This type of burial was only found rarely, used for special people. It was found out that these headless skeletons were both male and female.

Earlier I mentioned the wall paintings. Some of these paintings depict headless skeletons with the heads being eaten by vultures. James Mellaart had said that when the Neolithic people died, the vultures ate their bodies and the remaining bones would be buried in the houses. I found this explanation a little confusing, since the skeletons found during the excavations were complete. I think that if the vultures ate humans, they would scatter the bones around. So what are these wall paintings trying to say?

Now I want to mention the famous symbol of Çatalhöyük, "the Mother Goddess." It is a statuette of a woman who is fat and has got large breasts which symbolize her fertility. When one sees this statuette, one thinks that women were in charge within the Çatalhöyük community. But the latest studies suggest that this wasn't true. If the women were in charge, why did they feed themselves with herbs? For example, when lions hunt their victim, they eat its meat first and then leave the rest of it for the weaker animals. So, if the women were ruling the community, why did men and women eat similar amounts of meat? Also the headless skeletons that I mentioned before were both male and female and they were buried in a very special way. Did these men and women have some sort of importance within the community? All in all, I think the evidence contradicts the possibility of a maternal community.

Now we will visit the Visitor Center. There you will see copies of some of the artifacts that were found at Çatalhöyük. There are also information panels.

The thing is that Çatalhöyük is a very important site and I hope that you will find out about more about the discoveries that have been made here.

Dear readers, thank you all so much for joining me on my last guided tour of Çatalhöyük.

Afterword: Dialogue between Sadrettin Dural and Ian Hodder

Çatalhöyük, July 2005

Ian: I would like to start by asking you about the motivations that led you to write this book.

For hundreds of years many people have worked for foreign archaeologists in Turkey, the Middle East, and other parts of the world. They have worked, for example, as excavators and guards. On some projects there were hundreds of such people employed locally. But I do not know of any other case where one of these has spoken by writing and publishing. Usually their voices are unheard. Only the archaeologists, the directors, or team members write. Usually the local workers and guards have remained silent.

What do you think made you want to write? What motivated you to write, and why do you think no one has done it before?

Sadrettin: I started working at Çatalhöyük in 1993. I often felt intimidated by the knowledge of the excavation team. Therefore I tried to learn a lot from them in order to be like them. I did not know that no local workers in any excavation before tried to make themselves heard. Why did that happen? I honestly don't know, but I guess that those people in the past had not been given any opportunities to make themselves heard. People encouraged me. I am sure people in the past had the inspiration but were afraid or were not encouraged, or the people were not involved in the site where they were working. I became involved in part of the project so I wanted to write.

Ian: What made you think that your voice would be heard?

Sadrettin: We will all die at some point and some of us will never be remembered. However, the people who could leave some valuable knowledge for future generations would be immortal. My only strength is my pen and therefore I decided to leave a book for the next generations to become immortal and to live forever. James Mellaart came in the 1960s and became famous, then you came, and you became heard—why not me as a guard?

Ian: You talk in the book about sleeping at Çatalhöyük, often on your own. Do you ever imagine going to sleep and waking up at Çatalhöyük 9,000 years ago?

Sadrettin: I have never thought or imagined to go back to 9,000 years ago. Nobody believes that they could travel through time. They only wish that it would be possible. I really believe that there are many differences between now and the Neolithic times at Çatalhöyük. Why did the Neolithic people work less? Why did they live long once they had passed the first 10 years of their lives? How did they manage to live without arguing all the time? I think that they had a happy life. I am living in the present, but I am not as happy as them.

Ian: Is it important to you to imagine what life was like then? In the book you often describe your own imaginings and interpretations. Why is it important for you to do this?

Sadrettin: If we want to think about an unknown time, the best evidence is to imagine. I was quite curious when you first came because I couldn't understand why the work was important but I gradually understood why it was important. When that baby skeleton was found[1] I would go up to the mound at night and think about it. I was very affected by that. I felt I went back 9,000 years then. And then there was the example of the skeleton with the broken arm. I thought of the pain. I had a pain once. And then there was that man buried in the midden as if he was rejected, and I thought too of my own feelings of rejection, as when I drink.

Ian: Is the imagining a form of escape from the hardship of your life?

Sadrettin: I live for my dreams, but I have never hidden in my dreams to run away from my problems. The difficulties that I had were also a part of my life. Therefore I always tried to be strong even though I had many dreams.

Ian: Sometimes people say that the past is important because it gives them a sense of identity. Do your imaginings help you to have a better sense of yourself and who you are?

Sadrettin: Even though my past is important, I never tried to find my identity. But I do believe that I have an identity that might have been developed through my dreams. Before starting to work at Çatalhöyük I was a different person. Working here changed my identity and my dreams. It made me work harder and want to achieve something rather than just making easy money. I met new people and different things happened; it took me out of my routines.

Ian: You talk in the book about your poverty and powerlessness. You describe a hard life. But you also say that you love Çatalhöyük. Can you again explain why you love it?

Sadrettin: I had difficult days before I began to work at Çatalhöyük and it is true that most of these problems ended after I started working here. My father had a hard life and I wanted to escape that. However, my love for Çatalhöyük did not help me financially. And my work at the site did not give me higher status in the village—quite the opposite, really. One of the main reasons that I love Çatalhöyük is the attitude of the people who work here. Both the excavation team and the visitors never criticized my background, but respected me for myself.

Ian: The book shows you are a great story teller, and everyone knows that you like telling stories and making people laugh and smile. Do you think that is why you love Çatalhöyük—because it allows you to imagine stories? Archaeologists have to tell stories which they build from the data. Perhaps that is what attracts you to Çatalhöyük, also?

Sadrettin: I become very happy if I can entertain and make people smile. I believe that only the people who cannot smile know the meaning of smiling. I always admired the people at Çatalhöyük. If they dreamt, I dreamt. All in all these people helped me to develop myself as a person.

Ian: I now want to ask you some questions about the relationship between the site, the project, and the local community in the village.
    But perhaps I should start by asking you whether you object to the terms I am using—between local people and foreign tourists and archaeologists. I know from what you have said to me before that you have some ideas about the use of the term "foreign" to contrast with local or Turkish people.

Sadrettin: I never accepted the word "foreigner." Nobody is a foreigner in this world. In the past there were no continents or countries. There were a few settlements and a small amount of people living in the world. If there is anyone who agrees with the word "foreigner," they have to think about their past. In my opinion, we are all brothers and sisters and our ancestors lived in a social community. If we are their descendents, we must continue the social life style which they maintained.

Ian: Is it right to make a distinction between local people who live in Küçükköy and the global people who work at and visit the site as tourists? For example, your wife lived for 15 years in Germany and many people in the Konya area work or have worked in Germany and elsewhere. Is your "localness" real, or is it just an impression from the outside?

Sadrettin: I feel against any discrimination between the local people, the visitors, and the excavation team. We are all humans even though we come from different backgrounds. I am from Küçükköy. I was born, lived here, and am hoping to die here. I am not worried about being a part of Küçükköy. I am only happy to be a human. But it is true that some people in the village do not think about the larger world. They do not even come to Çatalhöyük which shows they are not really interested in the wider world. If they were involved in the site more, they would change.

Ian: Why do you think the site needs to be guarded? What is the threat as you see it?

Sadrettin: I think that Çatalhöyük definitely needs a guard. If the site doesn't have a guard, who is going to look after the visitors? Of course, another issue is the illegal excavations. Even though people nowadays understand the importance of archaeology and the archaeological sites, I heard about some illegal excavations at Çatalhöyük undertaken in the past—40 or 50 years ago before James Mellaart worked here.

Ian: What is the best way to stop people trying to loot archaeological sites?

Sadrettin: It is important to educate the people who are known to loot the archaeological sites. They should be told about the importance of the old settlements and the damage that can be caused by looting.

Ian: What sort of person from the village is employed on the project? Are they poorer and with less work?

Sadrettin: Yes, they are poorer people. And I think that you should employ the poorer people in order to spread the income around, but the people who work at the site sometimes give a bad impression of Çatalhöyük to the other villagers.

Ian: Has the excavation led to conflicts within the village of Küçükköy and in the local town of Çumra? Has the income it brings caused divisions within the village?

Sadrettin: I think those that work here try to protect Çatalhöyük, which has an emotional and financial value for them. There were problems between those who worked here and the people who didn't. For example, there were many people who wanted to work here and were not chosen. And there was this one guy who was fired because of a complaint by the other workmen. And there was a lot of concern about the women from Istanbul who started a Çatalhöyük craft center in a house in the village. The woman who set that up was using the place to trade and was taking money from the village.

Ian: Do you think the situation is better now because we employ people through the muhtar[2] rather than through an individual in the village?

Sadrettin: It is true that the workmen who will be chosen by the muhtar will be more trusted. However, I think that the elderly of the village should also be included in this process in order to control unnecessary arguments.

Ian: You talk very well in the book about the sudden silence when the team leaves at the end of each season. Our impact and contribution do not last long every year. What happens to people we have paid and supported when we leave? Do you think that the seasonal nature of the archaeology causes difficulties for those we employ?

Sadrettin: The reason that I mentioned the sudden silence when the excavation team leaves was to talk about the difficult times when they were away. The workmen carry on their own work after the season ends at Çatalhöyük. Some of them work on site as well as working in their fields after work hours. Everybody would want to work at Çatalhöyük the whole year round, but since it is known to be impossible, I don't think it causes any problems. People share the money they get from the dig with the rest of their family.

Ian: Do you think there is a link between the Çatalhöyük project and your court case? I know there is no direct link, but I wonder if there is an indirect link? For example, if you had not put so much money into the Çatalhöyük cafe maybe you would not have had to make deals that were risky. Do you think, looking back, there is any link like this?

Sadrettin: There is no direct link between my court case and Çatalhöyük, even though there may be an indirect link. The trouble would not have happened before I worked here. After I started working here I became encouraged by others to do risky things. At Çatalhöyük everyone works well together but we are naïve. I had no experience when I opened the cafe. I inherited money and sold crops to build the cafe and sold my house in Konya and the cafe has been a bad economic investment for me. But there is no direct link to the court case, though I also believe that if the excavation minibus didn't have an accident, I wouldn't have met the driver of the car and sold my car to him. He was the reason that everything happened to me. My cafe didn't cause me to put myself into trouble.

Ian: What do you think would be needed for you to make money now out of the cafe? Why do tourists not stop and buy things in the cafe more?

Sadrettin: I am losing money because of the cafe and may have to sell other fields. I think the visitors think that the cafe is expensive, since it looks it. Therefore they don't want to come. The tour guides should help by encouraging the visitors to visit the cafe. A price list for all the products which are sold in the cafe should also be placed somewhere visible by the entrance.

Ian: Do you think there is a way that tourism could be organized to benefit you and the village more?

Sadrettin: In order for the village to benefit from tourism, we could present both the village and the local people to the visitors as being nice and hospitable. This would help the village to develop culturally and financially. Some Japanese tourists came and walked around the village, and the village has gotten used to tourists.

Ian: If tourist numbers went from the current 11,000 a year to 111,000, would that be good for Çatalhöyük and for the village? Would it mean that other people would start cafes and businesses, and would you see that as a good thing for the village?

Sadrettin: In my opinion, more visitors are better for the villagers. Increasing tourism could help local people opening more businesses, which can benefit them financially.

Ian: I know that Çatalhöyük is important to the village of Küçükköy as there has been discussion of changing its name to Çatalhöyük. But in what way is Çatalhöyük most important for the village? Is it tourism and economic benefit, or is it education, knowledge, or something else?

Sadrettin: Çatalhöyük is situated in Küçükköy and I believe that it is important for the village both financially and educationally.

Ian: Who do you think should have ultimate responsibility for Çatalhöyük? Who should resolve disputes about which roads should be repaired, and where to build a museum? Should the ultimate responsibility be in the hands of the village or Çumra, or Konya, or the Ministry of Culture and Tourism in Ankara (as at present), or should it be in the hands of the archaeologists or even international bodies like UNESCO?

Sadrettin: I think that the Ministry of Culture and Tourism must be responsible for Çatalhöyük. I believe that they would always make the right decision about the site. The Ministry would be better in comparison to the others. Why do Çumra and Küçükköy want to have the proposed new Çatalhöyük museum—can they really care for it or is it just that they want to make money? If the museum is in Çatalhöyük then the Ministry would care for it.

Ian: If it is a private museum?

Sadrettin: This might work. I would like to make a copy of 10 Çatalhöyük houses and make a mini-Çatalhöyük for visitors.

Ian: I want to talk now about the relationships between you, the village, and the archaeologists who come here.
*   Do you think it is right that foreign archaeologists should lead a team digging Çatalhöyük, which is an important Turkish site?*

Sadrettin: It doesn't matter who is excavating such a site like Çatalhöyük. The most important thing is that archaeologists are excavating. Once tourists came here and asked me what I thought about foreigners and Turks working together, and in the past I felt that they would not be able to work together. But now I do not feel it matters who does the digging.

Ian: You and others in the village believe there are Yatirs in the mounds. Do you think that the archaeologists disturb these Yatirs? What happens when the archaeologists dig into the mound?

Sadrettin: Like everybody else, I also believe that there are Yatirs in the mounds. However, I don't know if the archaeologists disturb the Yatirs. We would have to ask the archaeologists if they had come across anything strange since they began working in the mound. If they weren't disturbed by the Yatirs, it means that the excavation team is allowed to dig here. You are always illuminating past history. Why don't you do research on the Yatirs yourself? Maybe you should go to the village and interview elders about whether such things really exist.

Ian: Archaeology is thought to be rational and scientific, and you say that some of your beliefs may seem irrational. But you also say that some of our behavior seems irrational. Do you think that we are wrong to say that local beliefs are less rational and important than archaeological science?

Sadrettin: I don't think that I mentioned anything like that in my book. It is true that 20 years ago the general behavior of tourists would not be accepted according to the customs of the village. But nowadays we are used to foreigners and people don't criticize the archaeological team. So we have developed in that way. For example, when you go to the village the women shake your hand and in the past that would not have been possible.

Ian: Do you think we should train local people more to be archaeologists? Should we teach them how to dig and record on

their own—as part of the team like the students and profession-
als? At the moment the people from the village who work at the
site have little education, and I think some cannot write. Do you
think they could or should be trained how to dig and record and
write? Do you think that would benefit them?

Sadrettin: I would be very glad if the local people would
be trained as archaeologists, since there is no age for learning. But even though they would be provided with many
opportunities, they wouldn't be as successful as the excavation team without any education. You educate children
at Çatalhöyük and most of them will go on to other pro-
fessions and it is important to increase their love rather
than to educate them. For adults it is good to train them.
I did not have any love for the site before I came to work
here. You need to be trained to love it.

Ian: I want to end by returning to the question of your writing
and your voice.
   Do you think that it is possible for you to have opinions
about Çatalhöyük that are independent of the archaeologists and
of the teaching that I and others gave you? I think you left school
at the age of 12, whereas many of us on the project have had
years and lifetimes of scientific training. Do you still feel you
have something to offer in terms of making sense of the site?

Sadrettin: It is possible for me to have opinions indepen-
dently from what I learned from the archaeologists. I still
produce ideas. Even though I don't have a high education,
I tried to train myself with the help of the excavation team.
I think that everyone can have their own interpretations
and ideas about the site, without being disrespectful. For
example, I had my own imaginings about that man with
the broken arm.

Ian: Many people who read your book will see this as the voice
of the poor and unprivileged writing back at the world that has

dominated them. People often ask if less privileged people have the power and resources to speak in their own voice. Do you see it like that; and how do you react to this idea?

Sadrettin: If the poor people who read my book want to be heard by others, I believe that they can achieve it. Some may think that I was lucky. In my opinion everybody creates his or her own luck. So I suggest the people who want to be heard should write and send it to some publishers.

NOTES

Chapter 1

[1] Konya is 42 kilometers from Çatalhöyük, a journey that takes about one hour by car.

[2] Erdoğan Erol.

[3] The Konya Museum is a state museum incorporating eight different museums in the town. Sadrettin is here referring to the Archaeological Museum.

[4] As David Shankland (1996, 2000) has shown, there is a belief among the villagers that the souls of the dead inhabit the archaeological mounds of the Konya plain and can be seen at night as lights traveling from one mound to the other.

[5] During the first seasons in 1993 and 1994 the new team conducted surface survey. Excavations began in 1995 (Hodder 1996, 2000, 2005a,b,c, 2006; Balter 2005).

[6] Osman Ermişler was at the time a curator at the Konya Archaeological Museum. David Shankland was the Acting Director at the British Institute of Archaeology at Ankara. The new project worked under the auspices of the Institute and David had kindly agreed to help set up the first season. Later he conducted ethnographic work in the village, published in Shankland (1996, 2000, 2005).

[7] In the early years of the project the team stayed in a building in Çumra provided by the local municipality (belediye). A dig house was gradually built at the site and the team was able to stay on site from 1996.

[8] Konya.

[9] The dolmuş is a common form of travel in Turkey. Somewhere between a taxi and a small bus, it carries groups of people at low cost.

[10] All men in Turkey have to do military service, which in recent years has lasted 1–2 years.

Chapter 2

[1] Starting in 1995, a dig house was gradually constructed at Çatalhöyük. Once complete it was able to hold nine laboratories and a Visitor Center, and could accommodate up to 80 people. The architect was from Konya Museum, and the builders were from Konya.

[2] During the construction of the dig house, the workmen built a small house for themselves behind the dig house.

[3] Çatalhöyük was discovered by James Mellaart in 1958 and then excavated by him between 1961 and 1965. After the excavations finished, a fence was built around the site and a guard established there. Before that time the site was used for picnics, gathering herbs, and for other recreation since it had not been used for fields for some time. Mehmet is probably talking about the period before the site was fenced.

[4] Until the dig house was constructed, there was a well just to the north of the East Mound at Çatalhöyük. It is probably to this that Uncle Mehmet is referring.

[5] In Küçükköy.

Chapter 3

[1] Shahina Farid started working on the Çatalhöyük project in 1996 and became field director and project coordinator in 1997.

[2] At that time the guards at Çatalhöyük were paid by the Konya Museum. Later they came to be paid by the project at salary levels determined by the Konya Museums.

[3] Sadrettin is right that there is much evidence of long-distance movement of objects to Çatalhöyük—shells and baskets from the Red Sea, flint, wood, and stone from the Taurus Mountains, shell from the Mediterranean, obsidian from Cappadocia (Carter et al. 2005). Ethnoarchaeology has been conducted in the Konya region in order to help understand Çatalhöyük (Yalman 2005).

[4] An example of Sadrettin's tour begins on p. 133.

[5] By "second hill" Sadrettin is referring to the north hill of the Neolithic East Mound at Çatalhöyük. As is clear from the tour described on p. 133, Sadrettin took people first to the South Area on the southern hill of the East Mound before moving northward to the second northern hill. Hasan Dağ is a mountain that can rarely be seen from the site far to the east in Cappadocia. It used to be thought that

Hasan Dağ was the source of the tools made of obsidian (a volcanic glass) found at Çatalhöyük, a conclusion now known to be erroneous (Carter et al. 2005). James Mellaart also claimed that a painting at Çatalhöyük depicted Hasan Dağ.

6 Karkın is a village about 8 km from Çatalhöyük (see map on p. 36).

7 A variety of "Goddess" groups visit the site as it is claimed to have a spiritual presence deriving from a goddess (see Bartu 2000, Bartu Candan 2005; Rountree 2001, 2002; Hodder 1999).

8 There are three or four guards who take turns staying at the site and guiding visitors around the site, the Visitor Center, and the experimental house. Visitors are not allowed to tour the site unless accompanied by a guard.

9 An *ağa*, or *agha*, is a local big landowner. So the name means "the agha's man."

10 An ox-cart with two solid wooden wheels.

11 Translated in English as a satan or devil.

Chapter 4

1 In Turkish the *hodja*, or *hoca*, is a Muslim teacher.

2 While James Mellaart recognized the mound at Çatalhöyük as Neolithic, it is incorrect to say that he discovered it since it was clearly known by the local inhabitants as one of the many ancient mounds in the region—see Salur and Ağa Adamı above.

3 When we surveyed the East Mound in 1993–1995, we found evidence of fields but could not date them. They looked relatively recent.

Chapter 5

1 The "garden" was a field used for vegetables opposite the entrance gate of the site. In fact, it turned out in later years that this field was properly owned by the State but seemed available because it did not have an identification or lot number.

2 This has become a common pattern in the Konya area, as perhaps elsewhere. In Konya itself, the shops near the main sites complain that the tour operators do not allow the tourists in the buses to shop freely in town. The tourists are given opportunities to shop at

specific outlets which have agreements with the tour operators. Sadrettin was a victim of the same process.

Chapter 7

[1] Every year one to three government representatives (*temsilciler*) are allocated to the field project, and in some cases these representatives come from the Konya Museum, as in the case of Osman Ermişler. Unusually, Osman bey was our representative twice, in 1996 and 1999.

Chapter 8

[1] Palaeo-environmental research (Rosen and Roberts 2006) has indeed shown an area of wetland around Çatalhöyük, with large-scale seasonal flooding caused by overflow from the Çarşamba River which ran by the mound. There is also evidence on site for the use of wetland resources including reeds, fish, water birds and their eggs (Hodder 2005a).

[2] Over the last two decades, large-scale irrigation schemes have been introduced to the Çumra area. These have diverted the water that used to run in rivers and canals into raised channels, and the effect has been a very dramatic lowering of the water table. The local farmers have thus had to bore their own wells ever deeper to obtain water. The marsh areas near Çatalhöyük have dried up and even larger marshlands to the east have disappeared.

[3] This description of Sadrettin's house is very close in its detail to what we have found at Çatalhöyük, although the materials differ and the walls are thicker than at Çatalhöyük. But it should also be noted that our understanding of the Çatalhöyük houses, our image of what they looked like, is already infused with our knowledge of the local architecture, so it is perhaps not surprising that Sadrettin can see so many similarities.

Chapter 9

[1] Obsidian is a volcanic glass that was traded over wide distances from Cappadocia in the Neolithic. It was used at the site to make tools, but also had a high social value. It is against site rules to pick up any artifacts from the surface of the mounds, as the surface distributions of artifacts can tell us much about activities and post-depositional processes (Hodder 1996).

[2] Erdoğan Erol, Director of Konya Museums.

[3] The *muhtar*.

[4] The evidence for this is animal pens within the settlement.

[5] See work on human remains (Molleson, Andrews, and Boz 2005).

[6] Molleson, Andrews, and Boz (2005) did not find extensive evidence of skeletal stress markers.

[7] There is only evidence for decreases in the area of settlement at Çatalhöyük in the uppermost levels, and even then much of the evidence can be explained as dispersal and fragmentation of settlement in the area of the site itself rather than out-migration or population decline.

Chapter 10

[1] A student from Selcuk University in Konya.

[2] Ayfer Bartu Candan worked on the project as an ethnographer (see Bartu 2000, Bartu Candan 2005).

[3] See Mellaart (1967).

Chapter 11

[1] In the Visitor Center.

[2] In the early Holocene.

[3] Certainly in the Çatalhöyük area it is possible to argue, given probable continuities onto the Chalcolithic West Mound, and the general expansion of Chalcolithic settlement in the area (Baird 2005) that population expanded when Çatalhöyük East was abandoned, and house types changed.

[4] I do not know how Sadrettin developed these ideas and interests in the link between himself and Neolithic peoples. He certainly knew that we were developing ancient DNA studies of the skeletal material from Çatalhöyük (see Malhi et al. 2005), but we were not asking population continuity questions. Many of the local nationalist politicians in the Konya region have picked up on the possibility of using modern DNA testing to try and demonstrate origins and affiliations, and it may be the case that Sadrettin was influenced by this development.

[5] See also Shankland (1996, 2000, 2005).

Chapter 12

[1] Designated times when the dig house and mound would be cleared of rubbish.

[2] Konya.

[3] We have at least managed to fund this suggestion of Sadrettin, and a parking lot was constructed in 2005 with the help of the local mayor (*belediye başkanı*). Other plans for the site can be seen by reading the Site Management Plan available at www.catalhoyuk.com.

[4] When we started working at the site in 1993, there were hardly any tourists. In 2005 there were 13,000.

Chapter 13

[1] Turkish Lira. In recent years the Turkish Lira has been revalued so that 1 new TL is worth 1,000,000 old TL with 1 new TL worth about US $1.20. There has been rapid inflation in recent decades but even at the time described by Sadrettin these amounts for the cow would have seemed very reasonable.

Chapter 14

[1] The store where the artifacts from the excavation are kept and sealed through the non-digging seasons.

[2] There is a grave marker stone that can still be seen on a small eastern hill within the Çatalhöyük East Mound (see surface surveys described in Hodder 1996). I do not know the date of the burial, but believe that it occurred decades before Mellaart excavated the site in the 1960s. The local lore is that it is the grave of a prostitute, and the digging that Sadrettin describes must have occurred before the archaeological excavations and before guards were posted at the site as a result of the excavations. The East Mound at Çatalhöyük had been used as a cemetery at least throughout Hellenistic, Roman, and Byzantine periods.

Chapter 15

[1] This is probably the BACH (Berkeley Archaeologists at Çatalhöyük) tent that was put up, with the aid of funding from the Friends of Çatalhöyük over Building 3 on the northern hill of the East Mound.

[2] This may well be David Shankland (see Chapter 1, Note 6) and this event must have occurred in the early years of our excavations.

[3] Muhtar.

Chapter 16

[1] Every year there are one or two press days at the site at which between 20 and 50 journalists are present. I have described my version of these press days and the particular event that Sadrettin goes on to recount in Hodder (1998).

[2] A bead from Classical times.

[3] Sugar beet.

[4] At the time, and to a lesser extent today, Deutsch Marks were used as a stable indicator of costs since the Turkish Lira was subject to very rapid inflation. Also, Sadrettin's wife had lived in Germany as a child.

[5] The *faraş ocağı* is a type of oven found in old houses in the region. It is located between two walls and close to the floor.

[6] The north hill of the East Mound.

[7] See p. 133 for an example of Sadrettin's tour of the mound.

Chapter 17

[1] Dr. Erdoğan Erol, the Director of Konya Museums, had his own office in the Mevlana Museum in Konya. The Mevlana is where Mevlana Celaleddin Mehmed Rumi is buried.

[2] We have so far only found one adult burial outside houses in a midden context. Most people were buried beneath floors in houses. The burial to which Sadrettin refers was of a young adult male (3368) who showed signs of "a gross systemic bone disease that affected most of the bones of the upper part of the body" (Molleson, Andrews, and Boz 2005, 295). The skeleton was not just lying in the midden but had been buried there. Burial outside houses is common throughout the Neolithic of the Middle East.

[3] There are no other obvious cases of exclusion, but we do now think that there was significant differentiation between those buried in the more elaborate and longer-term houses and those buried in less elaborate and shorter-term houses.

[4] A large number of child burials have been excavated at Çatalhöyük. Sadrettin may be referring to burial F. 464 found in 1999 in Building 17 in the South Area of the site.

[5] Theoretically it is possible that we would find another skeleton indicating the same parents as this baby, but in fact we have not been successful in extracting DNA from the Çatalhöyük skeletons.

[6] It is difficult to answer most of these questions of Sadrettin, much as I would like to, and much as many of them parallel standard anthropological and archaeological questions about post-marital residence and the like. Current tentative suggestions are that those buried within a house may have had some familial connection as seen from the repetition within a house of skeletal and dental traits that may be genetically transmitted (Molleson, Andrews, and Boz 2005).

[7] Sadrettin was confined in a small prison in the local town of Çumra.

[8] Shahina Farid, Louise Martin, Can Candan, Ayfer Bartu Candan, and Adnan Baysal.

[9] The word *hodja* refers to a Muslim religious leader.

Appendix

[1] Sadrettin is imagining here that the tour is taking place when Building 1 was still visible. It has since been excavated and the building beneath (Building 5) is on permanent display. There is some collapsing of time, since at the time that Building 1 was visible the shelter over the South Area mentioned earlier had not yet been erected.

Afterword

[1] In 1999.

[2] Village headman.

Bibliography

Baird, D. 2005. The history of settlement and social landscapes in the Early Holocene in the Çatalhöyük area. In Hodder, I. (ed) *Çatalhöyük perspectives: themes from the 1995–1999 seasons*. McDonald Institute for Archaeological Research/British Institute of Archaeology at Ankara Monograph, Cambridge. Pp. 55–74.

Balter, M. 2005. *The goddess and the bull*. Simon and Schuster, New York.

Bartu, A. 2000. Where is Çatalhöyük? Multiple sites in the construction of an archaeological site. In Hodder, I. (ed) *Towards reflexive method in archaeology: the example at Çatalhöyük*. McDonald Institute for Archaeological Research/British Institute of Archaeology at Ankara, Cambridge. Pp. 101–110.

Bartu Candan, A. 2005. Entanglements/encounters/engagements with prehistory: Çatalhöyük and its publics. In Hodder, I. (ed) *Çatalhöyük perspectives: themes from the 1995–1999 seasons*. McDonald Institute for Archaeological Research/British Institute of Archaeology at Ankara Monograph, Cambridge. Pp. 27–38.

Carter, T., Poupeau, G., Bressy, C., and Pearce, N. J. G. 2005. From chemistry to consumption: towards a history of obsidian use at Çatalhöyük through a programme of inter-laboratory trace-elemental characterization. In Hodder, I. (ed) *Changing materialities at Çatalhöyük: reports from the 1995–1999 seasons*. McDonald Institute for Archaeological Research/British Institute of Archaeology at Ankara Monograph, Cambridge. Pp. 285–306.

Hodder, I. (ed) 1996. *On the surface. Çatalhöyük 1993–95.* McDonald Institute for Archaeological Research/British Institute of Archaeology at Ankara Monograph, Cambridge.

Hodder, I. 1998. The past as passion and play: Çatalhöyük as a site of conflict in the construction of multiple pasts. In L. Meskell (ed) *Archaeology under fire: nationalism, politics and heritage in the Eastern Mediterranean and Middle East.* Routledge, London. Pp. 124–39.

Hodder, I. 1999. *The archaeological process.* Blackwell, Oxford.

Hodder, I. (ed) 2000. *Towards reflexive method in archaeology: the example at Çatalhöyük.* McDonald Institute for Archaeological Research/British Institute of Archaeology at Ankara Monograph, Cambridge.

Hodder, I. (ed) 2005a. *Inhabiting Çatalhöyük: reports from the 1995–1999 seasons.* McDonald Institute for Archaeological Research/British Institute of Archaeology at Ankara Monograph, Cambridge.

Hodder, I. (ed) 2005b. *Changing materialities at Çatalhöyük: reports from the 1995–1999 seasons.* McDonald Institute for Archaeological Research/British Institute of Archaeology at Ankara Monograph, Cambridge.

Hodder, I. (ed) 2005c. *Çatalhöyük perspectives: themes from the 1995–1999 seasons.* McDonald Institute for Archaeological Research/British Institute of Archaeology at Ankara Monograph, Cambridge.

Hodder, I. (ed) 2006. *Excavating Çatalhöyük: reports from the 1995–1999 seasons.* McDonald Institute for Archaeological Research/British Institute of Archaeology at Ankara Monograph, Cambridge.

Malhi, R., Van Tuinen, M., Mountain, J., Hodder, I., and Hadly, E. A. 2005. Pilot project: Çatalhöyük ancient DNA study. In Hodder, I. (ed) *Inhabiting Çatalhöyük: reports from the 1995–1999 seasons*. McDonald Institute for Archaeological Research/British Institute of Archaeology at Ankara Monograph. Pp. 307–312.

Mellaart, J. 1967. *Çatal Hüyük: a Neolithic town in Anatolia*. Thames and Hudson, London.

Molleson, T., Andrews, P., and Boz, B. 2005. Reconstruction of the Neolithic people of Çatalhöyük. In Hodder, I. (ed) *Inhabiting Çatalhöyük: reports from the 1995–1999 seasons*. McDonald Institute for Archaeological Research/British Institute of Archaeology at Ankara Monograph, Cambridge. Pp. 279–300.

Rosen, A., and Roberts, N. 2006. The nature of Çatalhöyük: people and their changing environments on the Konya plain. In Hodder, I. (ed) *Çatalhöyük perspectives: themes from the 1995–1999 seasons*. McDonald Institute for Archaeological Research/British Institute of Archaeology at Ankara Monograph, Cambridge. Pp. 39–54.

Rountree, K. 2001. The past is a foreigners' country: Goddess feminists, archaeologists, and the appropriation of prehistory. *Journal of Contemporary Religion* 16, 5–27.

Rountree, K. 2002. Re-inventing Malta's Neolithic temples: contemporary interpretations and agendas. *History and Anthropology* 13, 31–51.

Shankland, D. 1996. The anthropology of an archaeological presence. In Hodder, I. (ed) *On the surface: Çatalhöyük 1993–95*. McDonald Institute for Archaeological Research/British Institute of Archaeology at Ankara Monograph, Cambridge. Pp. 218–226.

Shankland, D. 2000. Villagers and the distant past: three seasons' work at Küçükköy, Çatalhöyük. In Hodder, I. (ed) *Towards reflexive method in archaeology: the example at Çatalhöyük*. McDonald Institute for Archaeological Research/British Institute of Archaeology at Ankara, Cambridge. Pp. 167–176.

Shankland, D. 2005. The socio-ecology of Çatalhöyük. In Hodder, I. (ed) *Çatalhöyük perspectives: themes from the 1995–1999 seasons*. McDonald Institute for Archaeological Research/British Institute of Archaeology at Ankara, Cambridge. Pp. 15–26.

Yalman, N. 2005. Settlement logic studies as an aid to understand prehistoric settlement organization: ethnoarchaeological research in Central Anatolia. In Hodder, I. (ed) *Inhabiting Çatalhöyük: reports from the 1995–1999 seasons*. McDonald Institute for Archaeological Research/British Institute of Archaeology at Ankara Monograph, Cambridge. Pp. 329–342.